WONDERFUL

A guide to Lahaina, Kaanapali, Kapalua and Iao Valley

Bob Abraham

As if emerging from the pages of history, these muscular Hawaiians paddling traditional outrigger canoes steer confidently across Maui's choppy channels.

TEXT AND DESIGN BY ANGELA KAY KEPLER

Mutual Publishing

Carpeted with mosses and ferns, the near-vertical walls of North Waiehu Valley merge to form narrow headwalls from which plummet many waterfalls. Their flows vary from trickles to gushing torrents according to immediate weather changes.

Library of Congress Catalog Card No.
ISBN 0-935180-63-X

All photos by Angela Kay Kepler unless otherwise noted.
Printed in Australia by McPherson's Printing Group

TABLE OF CONTENTS

ACKNOWLEDGEMENTS

Over the years numerous people contribute to the evolution of a book. To all who have expressed *aloha* to me—outdoor enthusiasts, business contacts, hotel personnel, musicians, friends and acquaintances from all walks of life—I extend warm thanks. Special gratitude goes to my father, David Brownscombe, for his invaluable help with domestic duties; the U.S. Fish & Wildlife Service; members of the Mauna Ala Hiking Club and Sierra Club; Bob Gustafson, Bob Hobdy, Derral Herbst, Stephen Mountainspring, Art Medeiros, and Mary Evanson for hiking and camping companionship under rugged conditions; Tom Hauptman of Pacific Helicopters, Inc. for some courageous flying; the Sheraton Maui and Maui Westin for superb accommodations; Bonnie Fancher and Patricia Provost for secretarial assistance and editing; Jim Luckey of the Lahaina Restoration Society; and to my children for their good behavior. Thanks are also due to my husband, Cameron, for his encouragement, proofreading, and companionship in the field.

Special gratitude is extended to all photographers, artists and organizations whose pictures enhanced this publication, and also to the late Colin Cameron, Sam Cooke, Maui Land & Pineapple Company, AMFAC/JMB Hawaii, Inc., The Nature Conservancy Hawaii, and Hawaii State Natural Area Reserve System, who are currently extending themselves to ensure that West Maui's precious flora, fauna and watershed be preserved.

David Davis

Lahaina Harbor and the West Maui Mountains beyond glow in a gentle rosy light.

P R E F A C E

*Peeking above layers of silvery clouds, the ridgetops of the West Maui Mountains are seen
here through a telephoto lens from the high slopes of Haleakala.*

From royal blue ocean depths, on through sandy and rocky shorelines,
over viridescent foothills and into precipitous mountain valleys, West Maui
offers a wide spectrum of enriching experiences and scenic beauty.

This book describes the entire mass of West Maui, beginning in
Wailuku and extending in a full circle past the historic town of Lahaina, the
prestigious tourist resorts of Kaanapali and Kapalua, and ending along the
rugged windward (north) coast. Each chapter corresponds to a particular
stretch of road (see map). Topics covered include accommodation,
agribusiness, art, beaches, birds, coral reefs, culture, dining, entertainment,
ethnic heritage, flowers, geography, history, hotels, snorkeling, and sports.
For street maps, phone numbers, restaurants and other specifics, consult the
current tourist guides.

Enjoy West Maui at each hour of the day and night, in the delectable
fragrances and hues of flowers, the sparkling interplay of sun and water, the
stillness of an early morning stroll on the beach.

West Maui has magical energies: light energy manifests as a rainbow
arching over an inland valley, wave energy curls in turquoise translucence
within sheltered bays, and wind energy shapes the cloud patterns over land
and sea.

Most potent of all is that captivating, impalpable energy—love. It
revitalizes us as we relax amidst beautiful, healthy surroundings. Feel its
energizing strength. Imbibe it...treasure it...share it.

Kay Kepler

5

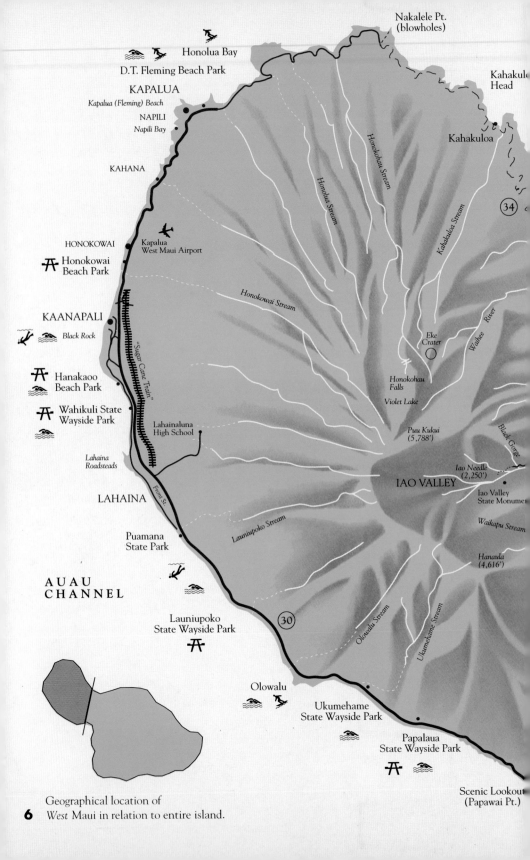

Nakalele Pt.
(blowholes)

Honolua Bay

D.T. Fleming Beach Park

KAPALUA

Kahakula
Head

Kapalua (Fleming) Beach

Kahakuloa

NAPILI

Napili Bay

KAHANA

Honolua Stream

Honokohau Stream

(34)

HONOKOWAI

Kapalua
West Maui Airport

Honokowai
Beach Park

Honokowai Stream

Kahakuloa Stream

KAANAPALI

Black Rock

Wahee River

Eke
Crater

Hanakaoo
Beach Park

"Sugar Cane Train"

*Honokohau
Falls*

Wahikuli State
Wayside Park

Violet Lake

*Puu Kukui
(5,788')*

Black Gorge

*Lahaina
Roadsteads*

Lahainaluna
High School

*Iao Needle
(2,250')*

IAO VALLEY

LAHAINA

Front St.

Iao Valley
State Monume

Puamana
State Park

Waikapu Stream

Launiupoko Stream

*Hanaula
(4,616')*

A U A U
C H A N N E L

Launiupoko
State Wayside Park

(30)

Olowalu Stream

Ukumehame Stream

Olowalu

Ukumehame
State Wayside Park

Papalaua
State Wayside Park

Scenic Lookou
(Papawai Pt.)

Geographical location of
West Maui in relation to entire island.

6

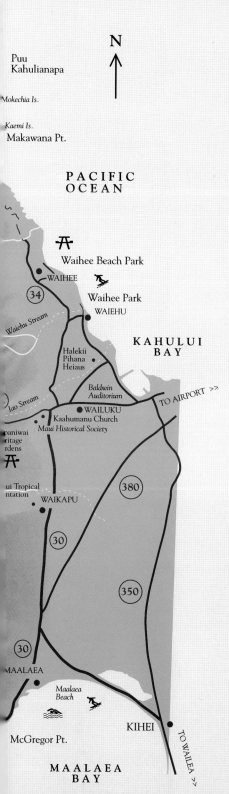

Puu
Kahulianapa

Mokechia Is.

Kaemi Is.
Makawana Pt.

PACIFIC
OCEAN

Waihee Beach Park

WAIHEE

Waihee Park

WAIEHU

KAHULUI
BAY

Halekii
Pihana
Heiaus

Baldwin
Auditorium

Iao Stream

WAILUKU

Kaahumanu Church

Maui Historical Society

TO AIRPORT >>

paniwai
ritage
rdens

ui Tropical
ntation

WAIKAPU

MAALAEA

*Maalaea
Beach*

McGregor Pt.

KIHEI

TO WAILEA >>

MAALAEA
BAY

Waiehu Stream

34

30

380

30

350

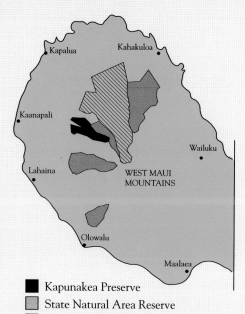

Kapalua   Kahakuloa

Kaanapali

Wailuku

Lahaina

WEST MAUI
MOUNTAINS

Olowalu

Maalaea

■ Kapunakea Preserve
▨ State Natural Area Reserve
▨ Maui Land & Pine Watershed

*With the addition of Kapunakea Preserve, an
uninterrupted area of more than 13,000 acres of
West Maui's watershed is actively managed for the
preservation of native species and ecosystems.*

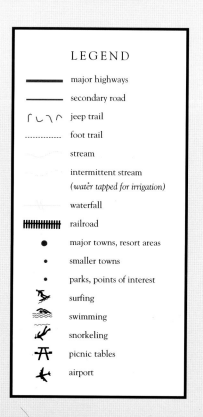

LEGEND

——— major highways

——— secondary road

⌐⌐⌐⌐ jeep trail

.... foot trail

〜〜〜 stream

intermittent stream
(*water tapped for irrigation*)

waterfall

railroad

● major towns, resort areas

· smaller towns

· parks, points of interest

surfing

swimming

snorkeling

picnic tables

airport

7

I WAILUKU

Wailuku (pron. "wy-*loo*-koo"), although an active business center and county seat (Maui County also includes Molokai, Lanai and Kahoolawe), still retains some of the sedate pace that characterized pre-statehood Hawaii (before 1959). Nestled on the alluvial fan spilling out from Iao Valley, it merges eastward into its larger and more modern twin city, Kahului (*right*). Life in its back streets is unhurried,

and many residents still carry on the family tradition of working with the land, a legacy of the old sugar plantation days.

Listen and watch carefully for living Oriental customs. You may see a group of elderly ladies taking a break from gardening, chatting in their native tongue, or an old man strolling home from the market carrying his daily bundles of taro leaves, imported Japanese seaweed, and *daikon* (a long white root vegetable like our cucumber).

Wailuku, gateway to the famous Iao Valley (pron. "ee-yow") is a charming mix of old and new. There are historic sites, ethnic restaurants (Thai, Chinese, Korean, Japanese), food to-go, cultural activities, lovely shade trees and a health food store. Here well-dressed lawyers mingle with Buddhist priests, "hippies," demure Japanese secretaries, and Filipino mechanics.

Wailuku (population 11,000) possesses a variety of architectural styles ranging from the nine-story County Building—so distinct you can spot it from the air—to tumbledown, tin-roofed shacks. Expansive mountain views offer a change from the ubiquitous Hawaiian beaches.

(*opposite*) Part of Wailuku's Historic District, **KAAHUMANU CHURCH** was named after the powerful chiefess and wife of King Kamehameha I, Queen Kaahumanu (1768-1832). An ardent promoter of Christianity, she owned the first New Testament printed in the Hawaiian language. After attending services in 1832 in a grass shack on the present church site at the corner of High and Main Streets, she asked that a permanent church be built and named after her. Unfortunately, the resulting adobe structure was poorly cemented and eventually dissolved in the rain. Today's charming New England- style edifice, with its steeple clock, dates from 1857. Its pews are made of *koa*, a prized native wood. Services are held by the Congregational faith, with hymns still sung in Hawaiian.

(top) The **OLD COURTHOUSE** (left) and **COUNTY BUILDING (right)** on High Street. The 10,000-foot shield volcano of Haleakala lies beyond. (left) Recent renovation of buildings includes **IAO THEATRE**, home of the Maui Community, and Youth, Theatres. Less than a mile away, the harborside Maui Community Arts and Cultural Center is under construction.

(above) The **MAUI YOUTH THEATRE**, recently moved from Puunene, continues to delight audiences with a succession of plays and musicals, providing opportunities for actors, young and old, to share their talents. Pictured are Maui teenager's Kirsten Frederickson and Eric Gilliom in a 1986 performance of Cinderella. Several of the island's talented youngsters, including Eric, have pursued successful acting and dancing careers on the mainland.

The **MAUI HISTORICAL SOCIETY MUSEUM:** Hale Hoikeike or "House of Display" (pron. "ha-lay hoe-eekay-eekay") is the renovated home of Edward Bailey (1814-1903), an early missionary, artist, poet, sugar miller and teacher. Set amid spacious grounds and mature shade trees, this museum imparts a sense of tranquility. It transports us to bygone days by way of missionary items such as 19th century furniture and handmade quilts, and artifacts from stone-age Hawaii, including tapa cloth, koa calabashes, and poi pounders. Special exhibits are presented periodically. Listed in the National Register of Historic Places, it was built in several stages between 1833 and 1850. Its 20-inch-thick stone walls did not suffer the same fate as the original Kaahumanu church, as Mr. Bailey knew the secret of adding goat hair to the mortar to act as a binding agent. The museum is located on the left side of Main Street (Route 32) as you drive up to Iao Valley.

(right) This old **CANOE,** built in traditional Hawaiian style from a single *koa* log, sits in an open shed beside the museum.

11

The core of Maui's year-round musical culture is the **MAUI PHILHARMONIC SOCIETY**, which presents a variety of classical, light and Hawaiian/ethnic music and dance. Through cooperation with statewide musical organizations, Maui audiences are able to enjoy the Honolulu Symphony and world-renowned artists such as pianist Vladimir Ashkenazy. The Society also provides educational music in the schools, artist-in-residence programs and summer music camps. Pictured is a scene from Tchaikovsky's "Nutcracker Suite."

An **OLD ORIENTAL COUPLE**, the late Wesley, aged 84, and Chyoko Wong, aged 73, respected *kamaaina* (old-timers) of Chinese and Japanese heritage, pose with home-pickled limes and a bag of Hawaiian sugarcane grown on their nearby farm. In families such as this, *sushi* (pressed rice wrapped in seaweed) and Japanese pickles are daily fare.

(opposite) Averaging 3,000 feet in elevation, Iao Valley's **JAGGED RIDGELINE** pierces the horizon in a succession of V-shaped canyons separated by buttress-like divides. This photo was taken from Route 32. The West Maui Mountains exhibit such steep topography because they are geologically very young: only 1.3 million years old.

12

II   IAO VALLEY TO LAHAINA

West Maui's magnificent mountains—a ring of precipitous, knife-edged ridges and deep, narrow valleys—are accessible only by Route 32. Eighty years ago, the verdant journey from Wailuku to Iao Valley took three hours; today a car makes the trip in about five minutes. Iao Valley State Monument, a six-acre park and botanical garden with views into the heart of the massif, is spectacular. Park your car, cross the bridge and walk up the steps to the Iao Needle Lookout, then stroll along the shady riverside trail. On clear days, the valley's headwalls and West Maui's highest peak, Puu   Kukui (5,788 feet, pron. poo-oo koo-koo-ee), rise in glorious splendor, marking the location of an extinct volcanic crater.

(*above*) A hiker's view from inside the dark valley east of Iao Needle, visible on the right from the staircase lookout. These **PICTURESQUE VALLEYS** have been carved out of volcanic rock entirely by streams.

Precipitous ridges seen from the mid-slopes of Iao Needle frame distant Iao Valley.

This delightful picnic area en route to the Iao Valley State Monument is maintained by the county as a tribute to Maui's multiracial society. Ethnic pavilions are dedicated to Filipinos (bamboo house), Hawaiians (thatched home, somewhat dilapidated), American missionaries (New England-style house), Portuguese (villa with arbor), and the Chinese and Japanese (landscaped dwellings). Picnic tables and barbecue pits are covered in case of rain (at least 75 inches of rain falls here annually).

The name Kepaniwai (pron. "kay-pan-ee-wy") commemorates the bloody defeat of Maui's chief, Kahekili—a pivotal event in Hawaii's history. In 1790, Kamehameha I, having begun to unite all the islands by force turned his gaze to Maui. Landing in Kahului Bay, he drove Kahekili's forces up into the heart of Iao Valley. Maui's brave warriors, decimated by deadly war clubs and spears of shark's teeth, fell by the hundreds, choking the stream and turning it red. The name Kepaniwai was thus born: "damming of the waters." The village downstream became Wailuku, "water of destruction."

Kahekili's son apparently escaped by scaling a 3,000-foot precipice at the back of the valley. This perilous "short cut" to Lahaina, the dream of many hikers, should only be used in a similar emergency.

The **CHINESE PAVILION** with ceremonial lions. Here is a memorial to Dr. Sun Yat-Sen, founding father of the Republic of China.

JAPANESE PAGODAS and stone lanterns commemorate the 75th anniversary of the first Japanese immigrants to arrive in Hawaii (1885); two life-sized statues of cane-field laborers were erected during the centennial year in 1985.

BLACK GORGE

BLACK GORGE, famed for its natural rock profile of President John F. Kennedy, is the last major side-canyon before you reach Iao Valley parking lot. Although there is some dispute over the Kennedy likeness, there is no question about the natural beauty of this impressive valley. During one or two hours of steady rock-hopping, the hiker becomes progressively dwarfed by breathtaking escarpments, which close in until they are only seven feet apart. Its vertical headwalls, rising 2,500 feet on both sides, are carpeted with velvety mosses and lacy ferns *(right)*.

To top off an exciting trek into West Maui's deep recesses, a hiker takes a short, brisk **SHOWER**.

A close view of a dripping bank of **MAIDEN-HAIR FERNS** (*Adiantum raddianum*).

(top) **IAO NEEDLE,** pointing its cathedral-like spire skyward for 1,200 feet above the valley floor and 2,250 feet above sea level, is the focus of the park. The "needle" is actually a rounded knob, the termination of a long ridge curving back into misty obscurity. The name Iao means "cloud supreme" or "facing the dawn." Since the valley faces directly east, the latter is especially appropriate. According to Hawaiian legend, Iao Needle is the pillared remains of a merman who was punished for seducing Iao, daughter of the demigod Maui (best known for snaring the sun up at Haleakala's summit). At right is a view from the lookout at the top of the steps.

(right) At the Needle Lookout, be sure to check the steep verdant slopes and dark valley walls for large (30 inches long) graceful white birds. **WHITE-TAILED TROPICBIRDS** or *koae-kea* (*Phaethon lepturus*), although fish-eating seabirds, customarily cruise around island valleys. They nest on inaccessible ledges in the cliff faces. The early Hawaiians occasionally stitched their soft, white feathers into cloaks, and their slender tails, used in courtship, have been highly valued for centuries. Even in 1900, a single feather commanded $10!

David Boynton

(bottom) Close-up of the similar **RED-TAILED TROPICBIRD** at its nest. No wonder island people once valued their satiny plumage!

TROPICAL TREES AND FLOWERS (some labeled) beautify Iao Valley Park and the nearby Tropical Gardens of Maui. Due to different flowering times, each week provides a new assortment. What beautiful epitaphs for the generations of *alii* (Hawaiian royalty) and warriors buried in this sacred valley!

The sweet aroma of **PINK PLUMERIA** (*Plumeria rubra*) is irresistible.

Curved, dangling triangles of reddish-pink distinguish the graceful heliconia, **RED COLLINSIANA** (*Heliconia collinsiana*).

Resplendent in tri-colored glory, the **HANGING LOBSTER CLAW** (*Heliconia rostrata*), originally from tropical America, dazzles the eye.

YELLOW GINGER'S (*Hedychium flavescens*) fragrant yellow and gold blossoms, produced annually by the millions, cheer roadsides and gardens throughout the state of Hawaii.

19

(left) The **LOKELANI ROSE** (*Rosa damascena*), Maui's official island flower, is small and delightfully fragrant but, unfortunately, rare. An excellent place to see it is in Iao Valley Park, on your left just before the first step leading up to the lookout. Native to Europe, the double-flowered *lokelani* (pron. "low-kay-lah-nee") was introduced to Hawaii in the 1820s by missionaries. Ironically, this "Maui Rose" is never plentiful enough to thread into longer leis for special celebrations; pink carnations and standard rosebuds are usually substituted. Here a pretty island teenager wears a *lokelani* head lei.

A **HIKER** pauses beside slippery cascades in Iao Valley's hinterlands.

A **LITTLE GIRL** enjoys the coolness of Iao Stream beside the lower trail. When water levels are low, you may splash and swim safely. After heavy rains the engorged stream becomes wild and dangerous.

(opposite) The **LOOP TRAIL** along Iao Stream is a pleasant, easy walk. The pale-foliaged trees with maple-like leaves are *kukui* (*Aleurites moluccana*). The early Hawaiians made medicine from its sap and candles from the nuts.

(above) Iao Valley shelters other extremely rare native plants, such as this purple-flowered **LOBELIA** (*Cyanea grimesiana*).

(left) Hawaii is full of surprises. While clambering around Iao's steep sidewalls in 1980, botanist Bob Hobdy rediscovered an "extinct" tree. This native, the **MAUI HESPEROMANNIA** (*Hesperomannia arbuscula*), bearing golden, thistle-like flowers, had not been seen since the 1860s.

(above) Hawaii's volcanic rocks, though appearing sturdy, are crumbly and porous, particularly on steep slopes. However, with extreme care, experienced hikers can enjoy "climbing" thrills. This photo shows the view from the **SLOPES OF IAO NEEDLE**. In the distant V-shaped slot lies the main part of Iao Valley.

(left) Viewed from the up-valley side, **IAO NEEDLE** presents a less imposing face—a mere bump on the end of a long ridge.

IMPASSABLE WATERFALLS and deep pools dot Iao Valley's network of streams. As the mountaintops contain very little flat land, heavy rains quickly cause flash floods and treacherous river conditions.

WAIKAPU

Waikapu (pron. "wy-kah-poo") village lies three miles south of Wailuku on Route 30 and is passed on the way to Lahaina beside the West Maui foothills. Here, amid a sea of sugarcane, is one of the most visited tourist attractions in Hawaii, Maui Tropical Plantation. The scenic backdrop to this plantation is rugged Waikapu Valley, whose topography, exceeding 4,000 feet in places, is similar to that of Iao. There is no road into the valley. Permission to hike upstream may be obtained from Wailuku Agribusiness Company or through the Sierra Club.

The plantation *(below)* boasts 120 acres of pavilions, orchards, crop fields and a nursery. Agricultural products on display include pineapples, sugarcane, papayas, coffee, macadamia nuts, and Maui-grown flowers and vegetables. The Agricultural Village also features aquaculture ponds, craft demonstrations and pictorial exhibits.

(left) Waikapu Valley's precipices harbor numerous tumbling **WATERFALLS**. Waikapu Stream formerly flowed into Maalaea Bay, but today almost all its water is tapped for irrigation.

An assortment of **MAUI'S FLORAL BOUNTY** can be found at the Maui Plantation, either growing in the nursery or as cut flowers. On this and the following page
are specialties from "upcountry's" cool, dry climate and warm, moist locations such as
Iao Valley and Hana. Dazzling flowers such as these form the basis of Hawaii's boom-
ing floral trade. Hotels, churches and many public buildings use island-grown flowers
in stunning floral arrangements, some of which reflect the ethnic heritage of their de-
signers.

Anthurium (*Anthurium andraeanum*).

'Jacquinii' lobster claw (*Heliconia bihai* cv.
'Jacquinii').

Dendrobium hybrid orchid.

Vanda orchids (*Vanda* hybrid 'Miss Joaquim')
en masse near Waikapu on Route 380.

Pink ginger (*Alpinia purpurata* cv. 'Eileen McDonald').

Papayas (*Carica papaya*) clustered on a palm-like "tree."

Sexy Pink' heliconia (*Heliconia chartacea* cv. 'Sexy Pink').

'Veldfire' pincushion protea (*Leucospermum* cv. 'Veldfire').

King protea (*Protea cynaroides*).

Pinwheel (*Leucospermum catherinae*).

MAALAEA

Situated in a sheltered cove on the southern edge of Maui's isthmus lies the fishing village of Maalaea (pron. "ma-ah-*lie*-ah"), only minutes from Waikapu. To reach it, drive Route 30 toward Lahaina and take the cut-off road at mile 6.

Maalaea Bay's natural harbor (now altered by a breakwater) has played small but significant roles in Maui's history. During the building of Lahainaluna School in 1831, the first secondary school west of the Rockies, the bay acted as a depository for logs dragged more than 35 miles from Haleakala's rain-forested slopes. From here, the logs were transported by canoe to Lahaina and upslope to the school.

During World War II, Maalaea and the adjacent "Gold Coast" extending south through Kihei, Wailea and Makena served as strategic training grounds for military activities. All amphibious maneuvers prior to the operations at Iwo Jima and the Marianas were practiced here. In those days, "Camp Maui" at Kokomo (near Paia) housed 16,000 Marines of the Fourth Division. Their fates were varied: some married local girls, some earned Purple Heart Awards, and some never returned from the battlefields.

Today, Maalaea's small boat harbor, once the site of an ancient Hawaiian *heiau* (religious site) and later a Japanese temple, consists of a row of beachside condominiums, a pair of restaurants, a fish market and a tiny store. It still manages to retain the pleasant flavor of an out-of-the-way fishing cove. Maalaea is one of the few mooring spots on Maui which provides year-round refuge for private vessels, fishing boats and commercial craft Charter boats are available here for whale-watching, sport- and bottom-fishing, snorkeling and SCUBA diving trips to Molokini, sunset sails, and other cruises. The early morning and late afternoon, when these tours head seaward, are the best times to enjoy the sparkling waters and distant views of Haleakala that Maalaea offers.

MAALAEA BAY, whose golden strand arches southward for miles.

(top) Though appearing perpetually idyllic, **MAALAEA'S BEACHES** become windy after about 11 a.m. each day. *(bottom)* One of the fastest, most exciting **SURFING WAVES** in the world, called "freight train," rises out of Maalaea Bay. This break, featured in several movies, looms up when a rare combination of southern storms, offshore winds and summer swells creates perfect conditions. To stay within its rapidly closing, oval "curl" without being driven onto the shallow reef requires a fast board and considerable agility.

Bob Hobdy

(top) A radiant dawn from Maalaea's pebbly beach.

(center) Early morning at Maalaea **BOAT HARBOR**. A U.S. Coast Guard vessel shares space with private and commercial craft. Maui, unlike Oahu, has little military activity.

(bottom) Most people assume that Hawaii's waters about with **FISH**, but this is not exactly true. You see plenty of small reef fish when snorkeling but such abundance is not typical . This shortage is due to overfishing and to the lack of shallow offshore lagoons that support large populations of fish. Most edible fish in Hawaii are caught in deep waters. Much "fresh island fish" is airfreighted daily from the South Seas and Central America. Maalaea, home of Maui's fishing fleet, is a good place to purchase fresh fish. In ancient times it is said that trained runners rushed newly-caught fish from Hana to Kaanapali (70 miles) so quickly that the gills still moved at the journey's end! Popular species are red *onaga* and silver *ulua* (pictured), dolphin fish (*mahimahi*), and tunas (*aku, ahi*). The latter are often eaten raw as *sashimi*, a Japanese delicacy.

MAALAEA BAY and Lanai, seen from the slopes of Haleakala, are dwarfed by celestial radiance.

(left) Around the corner from Maalaea is **McGREGOR POINT** (note lighthouse), very windy from the air.

PALI ROAD

Today's modern **PALI ROAD** (pron. "pah-lee," meaning "cliff") skirts the cliff faces for a few miles, gently descending to sea level. Its history is fascinating. The map name, Honoapiilani Highway, derives from the 12th century. More correctly Hono-a-Piilani, the name means "bays of Piilani." The particular bays (*hono* in Hawaiian) are six lovely ones north of Kaanapali, including Honokowai (a beach park) and Honolua (a surfing mecca). Piilani was either an early chief who ruled these bays or a heavenly maiden who travelled "by rainbow" from Maui to Lanai to visit her lover. The ancient foot trail, widened in the 15th century by another Chief Piilani, later bore carriages and cars.

Cameron Kepler

Seen from a canoe the *pali* (100 to 200 feet high) is well named. Do not attempt to clamber around on the rocks above or below the road as they are crumbly and unstable.

Highway tunnels are rare in Hawaii. There are two on Oahu; this, the **PALI TUNNEL**, is the only other public tunnel in the islands.

Pacific Whale Foundation

Visitors seeking respite from cold climates are not the only winter transients on Maui. Each fall, up to 800 **HUMPBACK WHALES** also migrate to the islands and stay until May. Whale-watching is a thrilling pastime, and for some a sighting may be an experience that resonates for years. Since whales remain submerged for only eight minutes, on the average, it is usually possible to glimpse the misty spout which signifies that a whale is rising to the surface to expel and inhale air (remember that whales are air-breathing mammals, not fish). Besides the spout, visitors might see a whale's huge black flukes, or a substantial portion of its 35-ton body. The rarest, most breathtaking behavior is a breach, where the whale propels its entire body out of the water, twists, then crashes downward again. Note the humpback's large flippers, largest of all whales, reflected in its scientific name, *Megaptera novaeangliae* ("big wing from New England"). Check at the resorts for slide shows or videos on whales.

James Hudnall

James Hudnall

James Hudnall

(above) These leviathans, sometimes reaching 50 feet in length, have traditionally chosen Maui's sheltered waters for **CALVING**. Mothers bear young every two years, after a one-year gestation period. Newborns, 12 feet long, weigh two tons at birth! They grow rapidly on their mother's creamy milk, produced at a rate of 100 to 130 gallons per day.

(center) This underwater photo not only indicates the relative sizes of man and whale, but reveals the unbelievable **ROYAL BLUE COLOR** of tropical ocean depths. It is important that humans disturb these whales as little as possible, since only about 7,000 remain in the world's oceans.

(bottom) **SCENIC LOOKOUT** (Papawai Point) at mile 8 provides a splendid ocean panorama that includes Maalaea Bay, Kahoolawe, Lanai and tiny Molokini. From November to May, humpback whales, spouting as close as 50 yards offshore, visit Auau Channel, straight ahead. Binoculars are always handy here. Neat, Hawaiian-style rock walls, remains of the original *alaloa* (a long trail which once skirted the entire island of Maui), can be seen upslope close-by. Several sections of the *alaloa* are currently being renovated by the State of Hawaii and Sierra Club.

33

James Hudnall

Humpbacks, like many Maui residents, have two homes: one in the islands and the other, shown here, in southeast ALASKA.

Cameron Kepler

In late spring Maui's humpbacks migrate north to the subarctic region, where ocean productivity far exceeds that of the tropics and subtropics. Here their thick insulating blubber allows them to feed and live comfortably in icy waters. Pictured is Aialik Bay, Kenai Fjords National Park, south-central Alaska in late June. Here the humpbacks share protected coves with orcas (killer whales), sea otters, several species of dolphins, the rare Steller's sea lions, and multitudes of breeding seabirds. What a drastic change from life on Maui!

Closely skirting the gentle ocean, this section of road, from which expansive ocean and mountain vistas can still be enjoyed, remains undeveloped *(below)*. A shallow, reef-enclosed lagoon at Ukumehame State Wayside Park (pron. "oo-koo-may-*ha*-may") is popular for snorkeling (miles 14 and 15). Maui's gentlest surfing break is at Olowalu (mile 16).

In 1790 Olowalu was the scene of the "Olowalu Massacre," a tragic event in Hawaii's history. An American fur trading vessel, the *Eleanora*, bartered for fresh food and water from the natives, the ship's lifeboat and its guardian were stolen. Next morning, the furious captain turned out all the native women from his boat, fired at a trading canoe and burned a small village. He then sailed to nearby Olowalu Village, where he offered handsome rewards for the return of his boat and watchman. They came—after a fashion—as a keel fragment and denuded thighbones. Further enraged, Metcalf planned a gruesome revenge. He encouraged the trading canoes from Olowalu to visit his ship, then ordered every gun and cannon to be fired, thus killing and wounding hundreds of natives. The sea was awash with blood and flesh. The event was christened *Kalolopahu*, "Slaughter of the Spilled Brains." Curiously, a few tragic murders have occurred at Olowalu in recent years.

Douglas Peebles

PAPALAUA WAYSIDE PARK (pron. "pah-pah-lah-oo-ah"), at mile 11, is representative of the many peaceful beaches—some sandy, some cobbly—that flank Route 30 south of Lahaina. Swim, boogie-board, fish, picnic or relax here, but beware of underwater rocks and *kiawe* spines hidden in the sand. Surfers call this beach "Guardrail." Drinking water is not available.

(top) A favorite time for traveling this relatively unmodified stretch of shoreline is **DUSK**, when offshore breezes create feathery rooster tails on the shallow waves, and the sun slips silently behind Lanai. *(bottom)* Different light vibrations during the day create moods that vary from soothing to glaringly bright. The ubiquitous **KIAWE** (*Prosopis pallida*) trees shed twigs armed with long, sharp spines.

UKUMEHAME CANYON, viewed from mile 13, is one of West Maui's most spectacular valleys. Its highest peak (*left*) sweeps dramatically to a height of 4,457 feet. For centuries, these foothills have been stripped of their original vegetation through the activities of men, cattle and goats, but the mountains and valleys beyond continue to inspire such visitors as this diarist, one Mr. Gilman: *"It is a scene of rare beauty, particularly at the time of the setting sun when the mountain peaks are in full flush of a coloring which is rarely excelled"* (*Thrum's Annual and Almanac*, 1907).

A helicopter view of **UPPER UKUMEHAME CANYON** shows the craggy, jumbled terrain typical of West Maui's massif. The shadowed ridge in the middle distance is famous for the daring escape of Chief Kahekili's son during the Battle of Kepaniwai (see Iao Valley).

Agriculture and tourism are Maui's major industries. **SUGAR**, a lowland crop, covers more than 47,000 acres on the island, 185,000 acres statewide. Botanically a tall grass, sugar is planted as stem cuttings, watered plentifully, burned to remove organic debris and harvested over a two-year period. *One ton of water is required to produce one pound of sugar,* so it is no wonder that most of West Maui's streams, tapped for irrigation, rarely reach the ocean.

During the 19th century, Asian laborers were imported to the islands to assist the sugar industry. Pay was poor and plantation life very regimen-ted. Cane-field labor was, and still is a hot, dusty, 14-hour-a-day job. Around 1900, a Japanese laborer earned $12 a month. Of this, it is said, $11 was sent to his family in Japan.

A **FISHERMAN** tries his luck at trapping small reef fish in the rocky shallows along Route 30. His circular nylon net is weighted along the edge with smooth stones. Before throwing the net, the fisherman pleats it carefully, then with lightning speed tosses it upward and outward. This traditional fishing technique is a picturesque reminder of life in old Hawaii, although today the rewards are meager. Early Hawaiians used numerous methods, individual and cooperative, to capture fish. Authentic nets, some of which are displayed in the Bishop Museum, Honolulu, were manufactured from fine threads of *olona*, a native nettle with strong fibers. A stain extracted from burnt *kukui* nuts helped prolong the net's life.

(left) From mile 14 to 16 are scattered beaches beside shallows enclosed by a barrier reef. These are good for novice **SNORKELERS**. *(right)* View towards Haleakala from a beach near the surfing spot locally dubbed "**THOUSAND PEAKS**."

(right) LAUNIUPOKO STATE
WAYSIDE PARK, pron. "low (rhymes with
cow)-nee-oo-po-ko," at mile 18, with silvery
sand, is spacious and restful. Its six acres of
lawns, beach, coconut palms and picnic
facilities include water, an outdoor shower
and a relative rarity on Maui, public toilets.
Its verdant character today stands in sharp
contrast to its desolate nature two centuries
ago.

(across) Inland of the sugarcane fields, West
Maui's valleys change character markedly.
Pictured here is shady **LAUNIUPOKO
VALLEY**, a few miles inland from the sunny
beach park. As Menzies traveled up-valley in
1794, he noted how he became *"embosomed in
a woody, deep, narrow chasm, with overhanging
black precipices of immense height on both
sides…difficult and dangerous to traverse."*
Obtaining permission to hike in all West
Maui's valleys is difficult and is best acquired
through hiking groups such as the Sierra
Club.

A distant view of **LAUNIUPOKO BEACH
AREA** from way up-valley. On the left is
Lihau Peak, 4,197 feet.

III LAHAINA

Lahaina (pron. "la-*high*-nah"), because of its geographic location, has long been a town dedicated to frivolity: a surfing and loafing "resort" for Hawaiian royalty; a lascivious playground for raunchy sailors; and, more recently, a surfing, loafing, shopping, pleasure-centered resort for international vacationers. The town's essential spirit still survives.

Lahaina is also rich in history, not only that of Maui but of the entire state. Since approximately 1100 the Lahaina-Kaanapali area has hosted noble families. It was the royal capital of the islands from 1802 to 1854, when Hawaiian royalty coexisted—not always peacefully—with lusty whalers and stern missionaries. In the latter half of the 19th century, Asian laborers, imported to toil on the sugar plantations, added distinctive cultural overlays. Because of the decline in whaling, by 1900 Lahaina had become a deserted village devoid of hotels. Today, East and West, old and new, mingle uniquely.

Lahaina (population 6,000), though only a few blocks long, is rich with remnants of past eras, thanks to the Lahaina Restoration Foundation, which, in the early 1960s, began the enormous task of restoring the town's historic sites. Lahaina has been a National Historic Landmark since 1964. Street maps are in all free publications including the small booklet *Lahaina Historical Guide*, to which the historic site numbers in this book refer.

Within Lahaina's limited boundaries the shopper may find a sensational assortment of both imported and island-made goods, ranging from the elegant to the vulgar, including art, clothing, jewelry, ornaments and food. Start early, armed with sunglasses, or you might wilt in the noonday heat. To reach Lahaina, turn onto Front Street from Route 30 at mile 19.

Lahaina's few **BEACHES** are private with obscure rights-of-way or none at all. Their waters are shallow and permeated with sharp corals. Kaanapali's golden strands are somewhat more accessible, although public parking is restricted.

A 12-foot-high BUDDHA, a replica of the noted statue in Kamakura, Japan (45 feet high, dated 1252 A.D.), was unveiled in 1968 to commemorate Japanese migration to Hawaii.

Cameron Kepler

43

Lahaina's famous Indian **BANYAN TREE** (*Ficus benghalensis*) is the hub of town. Park your car (if you can) and shop, visit historic sites, or explore the colorful harbor. Banyans, characterized by curious dangling aerial roots and multiple trunks, are common in Hawaii. This one (Historic Site No. 9 on Front Street near the Pioneer Inn) is of particular interest. Planted in 1873 to honor the 50th anniversary of the first Protestant missionaries, it is one of the world's largest banyans. Now 50 feet high, it stretches across more than 200 feet and covers two-thirds of an acre. In a town

whose name means "merciless sun," such extensive shade, complete with seats (*center*), is certainly welcome. A National Historic Landmark, this tree is fastidiously nurtured and shaped; *please discourage children from playing on it.* The name *banyan* was originally applied to Hindu merchants who spread their wares beneath such trees. How appropriate that every Saturday, Maui artists also display and sell items—paintings, photographs, sculptures—right at this location.

(*opposite*) Picturesque **LAHAINA HARBOR** is jam-packed with private and commercial boats. Charters are available for whale-watching or reef-viewing, sport fishing, snorkel/SCUBA tours to Lanai and Molokini, and sunset cruises. Turn *makai* (seaward) of the banyan tree on Front Street. James Michener, author of the epic novel *Hawaii*, once listed among his eight most cherished sights: No. 1, snow on the Big Island volcanoes, and No. 2, the small boats returning to shore as dusk falls on Lahaina.

A landmark of Lahaina, the **PIONEER INN** (Historic Site No. 8) is centrally located on the waterfront north of the Banyan Tree *(opposite, top)*. Although first built in 1901, too late to lodge whalers (who left 40 years earlier), the inn's present 19th century ambience and whaling memorabilia evoke a time when Lahaina's streets teemed with pleasure-seeking sailors. The original house rules included the following admonitions: "Women is not allowed in you room" and "If you wet or burn you bed you going out." The Pioneer Inn, whose popularity has not diminished since those times, still contributes heartily to Lahaina's nightlife. Lower photo depicts the inn around 1915.

Bob Abraham

Bishop Museum Archives

A glistening **PACIFIC BLUE MARLIN** (*Makaira nigricans*) comes ashore. Clothed in shiny metallic-blue with vertical stripes, this pelagic marlin is the most common billfish caught in Hawaii, inhabiting surface waters of the open sea, along with *ahi* (yellowfin tuna) and the famous *mahimahi* (dolphin fish). To try your luck in Hawaii, the "Billfish Capital of the World," charter boats are available from Maalaea, Lahaina, or Kona (Island of Hawaii). Summer months are best, no license is necessary, and boats supply everything. Most charters keep the bulk of daily catches, so if you want more than one night's dinner, filleted by the crew, make arrangements beforehand. On Maui, average marlin weights run 200-300 pounds. In 1986, an 874-pound black marlin (*Makaira indica*), winner of the "Lahaina Jackpot," was the third largest billfish ever caught on Maui. An increasing number of boats and fishermen these days practice "catch-and-release" in deference to conservation of the seas' diminishing resources.

PIONEER INN, viewed through the famous banyan tree.

Wailea Destination Association

Seaward of the harbor lie the open **LAHAINA ROADSTEADS**, whose easy access and relatively shallow, calm waters are suitable for pleasure boats—that is, until Maui's annual winter storms whip through. Between 1820 and 1870, this area was the prime Pacific anchorage of the American whaling fleet. When whaling was at its peak, an 1846 census of Lahaina listed 429 whale ships, 882 grass houses, 115 adobe huts, 59 dwellings of wood or stone, and 3,557 people.

Pierre of Lahaina Studios/Sugar Cane Train

Maui's **SUGARCANE TRAIN**, officially the Lahaina-Kaanapali & Pacific Railroad, opened in 1970 and is Hawaii's only operating train today. Reviving memories of Pioneer Mill's 19th century plantation days, its steam-driven locomotives transport passengers on a 12-mile round trip which includes a 300-foot rise in elevation. Its four coaches are designed after the "King Kalakaua coaches." Original rails from the old Kahului-Wailuku railroad were used in its construction. Photo shows the train chugging across the 415-foot-long Hahakea Trestle, 35 feet above a streambed.

48

Hugo de Vries

LAHAINA SHORELINE and roadsteads from the air today *(above)* and from the Pioneer Inn early this century *(below)*. The Lahaina seawall appears in both photos. The Pioneer Inn is the large red-roofed building beside the harbor entrance.

Bishop Museum Archives/Baker Collection

For those who have spent time at sea—within sight of land or amid a vast ocean far from habitation—the sight of boats reflected in calm waters and the salty breeze mingle to stir one's inner nautical longings.

Whisking along in a mild breeze off Lahaina roadsteads is a replica of an Hawaiian **DOUBLE-HULLED CANOE.** Unfortunately few details are known about ancient Hawaiian double canoes. Early Western visitors to the islands—explorers, missionaries and whalers—remarked casually that huge double canoes reached 60, 75 or 90 feet in length, but measurements are few. However, details of the elaborate rituals, omens, and spiritual preparation which attended canoe-making are better known.

Douglas Peebles

Cameron Kepler

Typical of seaports anywhere, Lahaina has its share of colorful **SEA CAPTAINS**. Cheery, weatherbeaten faces pop up everywhere—from the Pioneer Inn's porch *(left)* or a catamaran houseboat *(above)*.

Bishop Museum Archives/Baker Collection

An Hawaiian lady mends **FISHING NETS** in Lahaina around 1912. Note the traditional woven mats and "Mother Hubbard" muumuu, a legacy from the missionaries.

David Davis

Today a shopper's delight, **FRONT STREET** is one of the oldest and most historical thoroughfares in Hawaii. Though modernized, it retains a distinctly 19th century architectural style, due in part to its renovation for the movie "Hawaii."

Nakamoto Art Studio

FRONT STREET early this century. Soon after this photo was taken, a seawall was built to protect the road from winter storms. During the time of royal residency (16th-19th century), Front Street was called *Alanui Moi* or "King's Road."

Proudly adorning Lahaina Harbor is the grand **CARTHAGINIAN II**, a replica of a 19th century brig, epitomizes the nautical history of 19th century Hawaii. Imagine the Lahaina Roadsteads crammed with boats such as this and you'll have a fair idea of what Lahaina was like when it was *really* swinging.

The *Carthaginian I*, featured in the movies "Hawaii" and "The Hawaiians," ran aground and shattered on a coral reef just outside Lahaina Harbor as it headed for drydock in Honolulu in 1972. *Carthaginian II*, its replacement, has lived a busy, international life. Built in Germany in 1920, it was converted to diesel by Swedish owners, then for many years hauled bulk cement in the Baltic Sea. In 1972, when the Lahaina Restoration Foundation purchased the vessel, an all-Lahaina crew sailed her across the Atlantic and Pacific Oceans to Maui, where she was overhauled to become the only authentic, square-rigged brig in the world. Her "retirement" finds her as a floating whaling museum showing continuous videotapes of humpback whales and acting as a report center for whale sightings. *If you are interested in seeing whales, or have a sighting to report, do it here.* Incidentally, this brig is exactly the size of the *Thaddeus*, which carried the first missionaries to Hawaii from Boston. Imagine more than 30 people tossing aboard this tiny "ocean liner" for many months!

SCRIMSHAW. This ancient art of etching miniature pictures into ivory, shell and bone, was practiced independently by American Indians, Polynesians, Eskimos and bored sailors everywhere. Waiting lovers, fantasies and maritime topics remain its primary themes. During the grand whaling era, scrimshanders used nails for outlining, sail needles or jack knives for carving, small chisels for inlaying, lamp black for staining, sharkskin for smoothing and sailmaker's wax for polishing. Although modern scrimshaw is highly professional, old pieces, many valuable, carry a high sentimental value. Life at sea was bitterly hard—food and pay were miserable, the stench of dead whales was nauseating, and sickness was common. After years of hard work, most sailors had little more than a few souvenirs, a weak body, ragged clothes and some hand-carved whale's teeth.
Lahaina is today a world center for scrimshaw; products range from tiny charms to heirloom investments. Since 1973, when the importation of whale products to the U.S. was banned, fossil ivory has become a favored medium for engravings. Some walrus teeth are 2,000 years old, while mastodon tusks extend back 50,000 years. Martin Bandy's work (pictured) is noted for its intricate details conveying facial expressions, postures and moods.

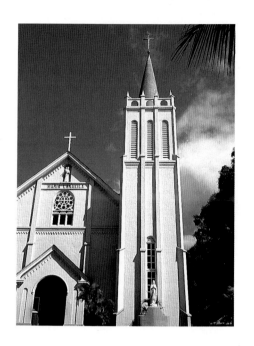

(left) **MARIA LANAKILA CHURCH**, Historic Site No. 26, the oldest Catholic church on Maui, is a concrete replica of a wooden house of worship erected in 1828. It is located at the corner of Wainee and Dickenson Streets. The first Catholic priest arrived on Maui in 1846, much to the consternation of the Protestant missionaries who thought they were doing a fine job of converting the "heathen" to their own faith. During the next few decades, thousands of Portuguese and Filipino Catholics arrived, swelling the numbers of Catholic converts. Today, Catholicism is the largest Christian denomination in the state. Note the Madonna's flower lei—only in Hawaii!

(right) "'This is beastly!' I heard one man remark as he climbed out of his berth. 'Waked up at one o'clock in the morning to go ashore, and not find a single hotel where one can get accommodation.'" So complained an 1890s traveler to Lahaina who was visiting various spots on Maui via steamer vessel (in *Hawaii…Our New Possessions* by J. R. Musick, 1898). Today's situation is greatly improved, although Lahaina has limited accommodations compared to Kaanapali and resorts further north. The Pioneer Inn has already been mentioned with regard to historical sites. Next to 505 Front Street, a New England-style shopping plaza, is **LAHAINA SHORES**, a large moderately priced, waterfront hotel that sports an enormous Hawaiian flag. The curious juxtaposition of the British Union Jack and the American flag reflects Hawaii's legacy of explorers from these two empires.

A **COCONUT PALM SUNSET** always adds an element of romance and delight to one's day. Enjoy every moment. Grab your camera and your special friend's hand, as tropical sunsets, often advertised as lingering, are very ephemeral. They typically occur between 6 and 7:30 p.m. At right, apricot and royal blue skies coalesce into a gently blazing backdrop to the twinkling **"CARTHAGINIAN II."**

Pierre of Lahaina Studios/Lahaina Restoration Foundation

BALDWIN HOME, a residence of the Reverend and Mrs. Dwight Baldwin from 1838 to 1871, is now a delightfully authentic museum. This stately family home, donated to Maui by family heirs, pays homage to all missionaries in Hawaii. It is centrally located on a shady corner of Front Street near the banyan tree.

On display are paintings, family treasures, period furniture, an antiquated medical kit, a piano with hymnbook (*right*), and everyday articles. A busy missionary and physician, Baldwin was also intimately involved in community affairs. He was a primary force in controlling the "sinful" antics of whalers and in educating the "natives" in practical and religious matters. As befitted his community position, he also hosted Hawaiian royalty, visiting dignitaries and ship's captains.

In Hawaii, the Baldwin name is synonymous with missionaries and success. Beginning with Baldwin's own six children, the family's descendants have become prominent in island business, agriculture, ranching, commerce, tourism, and philanthropy. The Alexander and Baldwin Company is so well known it is listed in the phone directory as "A&B"!

By 1852, lawlessness had grown to such a degree that the Old Fort (**below**) was sorely inadequate. Using coral blocks stripped from the fort, prisoners built a high wall around a small wooden structure (**above**), the **OLD PRISON**, *Hale Paahao* ("House Stuck in Irons"). Offenses leading to imprisonment included ship desertion, drunkenness, and dangerous horse riding. Fines were stiff. For example, a list from 1844 runs thus: $10 for "lewd, seductive and lascivious conduct," $50 for rape, $6 for "desecrating the Sabbath" and $10 for "coming ashore with a knife, swordcane or any other dangerous weapon." Relative to salaries, such prices for misconduct were exorbitant. For *four years' work*, a captain received the grand sum of $380, while at the lower end of the scale, a cabin boy pocketed a mere $28.

(**left, opposite center**) The **OLD FORT** (Historic Site No. 11), on the waterfront, is an authentic-looking 1960s reconstruction of a fort that existed between 1832 and the 1850s. Composed of coral blocks hewn from the nearby reef, it was 20 feet high and enclosed one acre of ground. The fort was built by royal command during the whaling era when unruly behavior was rife. At one time, 47 cannons sat atop its walls. The original fort was disassembled to construct a larger compound, the Old Prison (**above**).

(*above*) If it were not for the lusty **WHALERS**, this little town would not have needed all its prisons, forts, stiff rules, and punishments. Notice, though, that the whales in the painting are sperm whales (a type of toothed whale), which were the *raison d'etre* of the whaling industry. Sperm whales are cold-water species, most common off Japan. Hawaii's humpback whales were only a small part of the whaling industry, and even though Lahaina had a few shore-based whaling stations, humpbacks were rarely taken.

(*center*) The remains of Lahaina's **OLD FORT** guard the south corner of Canal Street, *makai* of the banyan tree.

(*left*) The **COURT HOUSE**, next to the fort, faces the harbor. It was built in 1859 to house a court, a jury room, and government and customs offices. An earlier, tin-roofed building had been destroyed by furious winds whipping from the north coast, over West Maui's topmost ridges, and down Kauaula Valley (the valley directly behind Lahaina) to Lahaina town. Such destructive weather is most unusual; normally Lahaina is calm and hot, except for occasional winter storms from the south.

The first Chinese immigrants came to Hawaii as sandalwood merchants around 1800, well before the missionaries and whalers. Fifty years later, larger waves of Chinese were imported as sugar plantation laborers. The **WO HING TEMPLE**, Historic Site No. 29, originally built in 1912 and fastidiously renovated in 1983, is a fascinating museum. It is located just north of the junction of Front Street and Lahainaluna Road. Today Maui has an extremely small Chinese population compared to Oahu. Japanese (20%), Hawaiian and part-Hawaiian (26%), *haoles* or Caucasians (25%) and Filipinos (16%) are the major ethnic groups.

Twenty feet away from bustling, tourist-oriented Front Street, a calm Oriental room is dominated by an orchid-decorated Buddha. **HANGING LANTERNS (*right*)**, a **METALLIC CANDLE (*left*)**, and numerous artifacts—all *so Chinese*. Is this Lahaina?

(*above*) A corner of the Wo Hing Temple's **CHINESE KITCHEN**.

(*below*) Many miles of **IRRIGATION DITCHES AND TUNNELS** honeycomb West Maui's rugged mountains. Most were hand-chipped out of solid rock by Chinese laborers. They skirt deep ravines and precipitous cliffs, serving as monuments to these early immigrants who helped weave Hawaii's present cultural, social and agricultural fabric. Photo shows the author, with headlamp, emerging from a long water tunnel high above Honokohau Valley.

Cameron Kepler

BUDDHA, holding a lotus, symbol of enlightenment, is an important figure to all Orientals.

An old, zither-like Chinese **MUSICAL INSTRUMENT**.

The meticulously-tended Lahaina Jodo Mission Cultural Park contains the **BUDDHA** (*left and below*), a **PAGODA,** holding ashes of the deceased (*right*), a gong, a cemetery and a Japanese temple.

(*left*) During summer, a colorful event is the **BON DANCE** featuring *taiko* drums and dancers dressed in *kimonos*. A special ceremony involves hundreds of tiny "candle-boats" floating out to sea at sunset, lighting the journey of souls to Nirvana, the land of bliss. Further ceremonies and dances honor Buddha's birthday in early April at all Buddhist temples in the state. (*right*) A close-up view of the Pagoda's **INTRICATE WOODWORK.** If it were not for the coconut palm and rainbow shower tree, both tropical, one might think this photo was taken in Japan.

(left) An elaborately-painted ceiling and **FLOWER-DECKED ALTAR** adorn the Japanese temple.

Across the road from the mission park sits a **CEMETERY** within the sand dunes.

Another Japanese custom greets you at almost every doorstep in Hawaii; island residents are horrified when you walk into their houses with shoes on! Incidentally, locals call flip-flops "slippers."

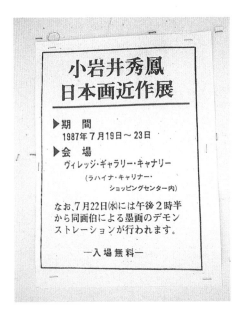

Traditional Japanese flower arranging (*ikebana*) thrives throughout Maui, but especially in the older residential areas of Lahaina, Kahului and Wailuku. Generally associated with Buddhist Church groups, it is mostly taught and practiced by those who emigrated from Japan decades ago. Photo shows white chrysanthemums (symbol of October) and local Christmasberry. *Ikebana*'s underlying philosophy is based on a love for, and respect of, Nature.

The Japanese language is still alive in Lahaina as well as in Wailuku. This poster advertises a **JAPANESE PAINTING EXHIBITION** by Shuho Koiwai, held between July 19 and 23, 1987. The bottom line reads "All are Welcome."

64

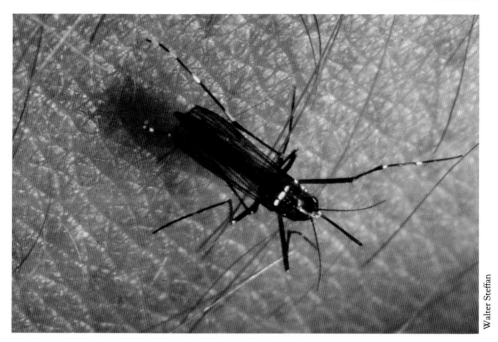

Walter Steffan

MOSQUITOS, the pesky little insects that inhabit Hawaii from sea level to around 3,500 feet elevation, may be appropriately mentioned here. In 1826, the crew of the whaling ship *Wellington*, returning to Lahaina to hunt women and alcohol, confronted new laws and fines for misdemeanors. According to the Hawaiian chief and missionaries, there were to be no grog shops, no brothels and not even any women swimming out to the ships! Enraged, the sailors emptied a water cask, last filled in Mexico, into a freshwater stream like the one above. Within this cask lived larvae of the Mexican night-flying mosquito (*Culex quinquefasciatus*). From that fateful date, mosquitos have bitten every resident and visitor to the Hawaiian Islands. There are now five species of mosquitos in Hawaii that bite humans, none of which transmit diseases. However, they do carry avian malaria, a disease similar to human malaria that is lethal to birds. This has played such havoc with Hawaii's native bird populations that, along with forest destruction and introduced mammals, *20 percent of the world's extinct birds were from Hawaii.*

(*above*) This very early, undated photo, entitled "**LAGOON-MARSH, LAHAINA,**" shows one of the many lakes, marshes, and streams which enriched Lahaina's shoreline before the advent of sugar agribusiness. The **TRANQUIL STREET** scene (*below*) is also undated.

In 1831, **LAHAINALUNA HIGH SCHOOL**, the first high school west of the Rockies, was founded. Its first students were Hawaiian, and all instruction and textbooks were in Hawaiian. In addition to studying, the pupil's activities included farming, phoneticizing the Hawaiian language, compiling Hawaiian dictionaries and operating Maui's first printing press. This respected school still emphasizes Hawaiian culture. Its grounds are shaded with mature trees, including an elegant entryway of royal palms. David Malo Day, honoring an early Hawaiian scholar, is celebrated each spring. To reach the school, turn north at the sugar mill at mile 20 on Route 30. The large white "L" on the hill behind Lahaina represents Lahainaluna and is limed twice a year by students.

PIONEER SUGAR MILL is one of three active mills on Maui. Sugarcane is refined only to the raw (demerara) sugar stage, at which it looks like translucent tan granules. It can be found in most markets and in small brown packets on restaurant tables. Further processing to white sugar takes place in California. Maui produces two percent of the sugar consumed in the U.S. The mill location is at mile 20, Route 30—you cannot miss the smokestacks.

Lahaina is ablaze with color, especially during summer. These pages show trees that are particularly common in Lahaina.

(*left*) Brilliant partners, **ALLAMANDA** flowers (*Allamanda cathartica*) and **CROTON** leaves (*Codiaeum variegatum*) have long beautified island gardens, thriving in bright sunshine.

Maui Inter-Continental Hotel

The light papery **SEEDPODS** of the African tulip tree (*above*) are occasionally fashioned into unusual leis.

(*right*) **AFRICAN TULIP TREES** (*Spathodea campanulata*), along with plumerias, palms and assorted tropical ornamentals, can be seen in the Lahaina-Kaanapali area. These dark-foliaged trees also mingle with lush lowland foliage along the Hana Highway. (*lower right*) Year-round clusters of brilliant "TULIPS" characterize this handsome tree which is easily recognizable from a distance. Native to tropical Africa and unrelated to true tulips, the dazzling orange flowers resemble lopsided originals from Holland.

(**center**) An 1820s prediction for Lahaina by resident C. S. Stewart has come true: *"The taste, skill and industry of an American gardener might convert it into an earthly Paradise; but now every where (sic) appears only like the neglected grounds of a deserted plantation."* One of Lahaina's most common trees today, shading even the smallest backyards, is the **MANGO** (*Mangifera indica*). Lahaina's "merciless sun" ripens its fruits into super-sweet, orange, finger-licking delectables, not to be missed from May to July. Varieties "Haden" and "Pirie" are best.

(**left**) Lahaina is one of the hottest, driest spots in the islands. The West Maui Mountains almost completely obstruct the cooling influence of the island's northeast trade winds, leaving this part of Maui to bake in leeward aridity. Most of the streams are tapped for domestic water and irrigation. **BOUGAINVILLEA** (*Bougainvillea* species) thrives in this climate. This well-pruned hedge is trimmed neatly to encourage a brilliant display of color.

(**left**) Unknown in the wild state, **LYCHEES** (*Litchi chinensis*), native to southern China and cultivated to more than 2,000 years in Asia, were introduced to Hawaii in 1873 by Chinese immigrants. To fruit abundantly, lychee trees need full sun, ample water and wind protection, conditions met in Lahaina. When they are in season (summer), the trees literally droop with generous clusters of crimson, rough-skinned (almost prickly) fruit, during which time they are usually available in supermarkets. Inside their thin shell lies a deliciously sweet, white-translucent, juicy pulp, reminiscent of grapes in texture and flavor.

ART IN LAHAINA

Art is one of Lahaina's specialties. West Maui is a focus for painters, sculptors, photographers, potters, wood-carvers, silkscreeners, weavers, and other artists. Themes vary from old-time and present-day Hawaiian scenes to contemporary subjects indirectly inspired by Hawaii. The variety of media utilized is staggering. In recent years marine subjects have become popular: reef fish, marine mammals, and paintings depicting split underwater and terrestrial perspectives. Well-known names are George Allen, Stephen Burr, Joyce Clark, Larry Dotson, Betty Freeland, Marian Freeman, Jan Kasprzycki, Fred Ken Knight, Lowell Mapes, Robert Nelson, Macario Pascual, Richard Pettit, and Cecelia Rodriquez. Many other Hawaiian artists present periodic shows and/or display their works permanently in West Maui Galleries. Those with particularly unique styles are Herb Kane, Peggy Hopper, Phan Barker, Patrick Ching, and Louis Pohl. The Old Jail Gallery, in the Courthouse basement, presents continuous shows by local artists. Don't forget the outdoor displays beneath Lahaina's banyan tree on Saturdays!

Wailea Destination Association

Hawaiian artist Herb Kawainui Kane is indispensable in preserving a pictorial awareness of ancient times. Every detail is culturally and geographically accurate. Here he has recreated a village scene at Kekaa, the present location of Kaanapali resort. An auspicious omen, a rainbow, hovers over the West Maui foothills. In bygone days rainbows acted as bridges connecting the heavens and earth or spanning different islands, thus allowing unrestricted travel of humans, gods, and demigods.

Village Gallery, Lahaina

Village Gallery, Lahaina

Betty Hay Freeland, a Lahaina resident descended from Hawaiian royalty, paints Hawaii as she remembers it from childhood and her extensive hiking experiences. Her oil paintings (also botanically and geographically correct) capture the subtle nuances and fleeting qualities of light. She excels at portraying the *élan* of Hawaii's natural areas and surrounding seas. (*top*) Maalaea Bay and the West Maui Mountains from Ulupalakua Ranch (3,500 feet) on Haleakala; (**bottom**) "Kapalua Morning."

Village Gallery, Lahaina

George Allen, originally from Australia, is well-traveled. Lahaina has been his home since 1973, from which he has immersed himself in capturing the vitality of Hawaii's coasts, flowers, and scenery. One of his specialties is Lahaina harbor. (*top*) "Early Morning Welcome—Lahaina"; (*bottom*) "Kiko's Canoe—Punaluu," a moment in time from the Island of Hawaii.

Marian Freeman, originally from Utah, has also lived in Lahaina since 1973. A very creative artist, she frequently heightens her colorful paintings with the blue end of the spectrum. Her anthuriums writhe with vibrant movement; (**right**) a pointillism technique imparts restfulness to an upcountry cottage.

Marian Freeman/Village Gallery

Marian Freeman/Village Gallery

Richard Pettit/Coast Gallery

Richard Pettit, one of the top marine artists in the world, is a native of Louisiana but has lived in Hawaii since 1982. His love of the ocean and watercolors have geared his artistic specialization to marine life. His fish, characterized by bold colors and perky personality, are anatomically precise even though Pettit enjoys taking liberties with their natural coloration.

IV CENTRAL RAIN FORESTS

If Lahaina and Kaanapali are scorching hot and dry, the opposite is true of the verdant mountains visible from their shores. Only a few miles inland from the popular beaches lies a world of fabulous cascades, dripping mossy forests and soggy bogs harboring an impressive list of 127 plant/wildlife/ecosystem types, 30 of which are found nowhere else on earth. Largely inaccessible, here lie fragile ecosystems where daily rain feeds numerous waterfalls which plunge more than 1,000 dizzying feet into deep ravines. Early travelers raved over their beauty: "[The mountains were] *rocky and precipitous, torn by deep shadowy ravines and cavernous gorges. Many who have traveled extensively for the sake of observing natural scenery declare they have never seen mountains which in variety and form, coloring and beauty, exceed the mountains of Maui*" (*Hawaii...Our New Possessions*, 1898, by John Musick).

West Maui's interior massif is scarcely a range of mountains in the accepted sense. It more resembles an irregular circle of steep valleys and knife-edged ridges radiating, like wheel spokes, from several central boggy flats. Puu Kukui, 5,788 feet high, and West Maui's highest point, is also not a true peak but the topmost bog on a spectacular cloud-hugging ridge which forms the mountain's "backbone." The photo below was snapped over Puu Kukui, looking north to another major bog and isolated plateau, Eke Crater (4,480 feet).

Two reasons why these mountains and valleys are so sharply precipitous are because they are geologically very young (1.3 million years old) and they receive copious rains. Heavy rainfall also means that when the vegetative cover is disturbed or removed, serious erosion takes place causing silty runoff which kills the offshore coral reefs. Vital subterranean and surface water reserves then become severely depleted.

As a result of such concerns, in 1990, the State of Hawaii, The Nature Conservancy Hawaii, and Maui Land & Pineapple Company signed a joint agreement to protect 13,000 acres of critical watersheds. This includes the new Kapunakea Preserve (1,200 acres) and four Natural Area Reserves: Honokowai Kahakuloa and Eke Crater, Lihau, and Panaewa (6,702 acres). Ridding these areas of feral pigs, fencing bogs and controlling alien weeds and erosion is a gargantuan, expensive task, but is imperative for the continuation of West Maui's ecosystems and agriculture, and for the quality of life of Maui's human residents and visitors.

A hiker's view of the fabulous, double-tiered HONOKOHAU FALLS, 1,120 feet high, is the loftiest perennial, named waterfall on Maui. It presides over West Maui's heart at the head of Honokohau Valley.

From 1977 to 1988 the U.S. Fish & Wildlife Service conducted comprehensive forest surveys on all the Hawaiian Islands, including West Maui. This baseline biological inventory pinpointed certain areas needing fencing, hunting, weed control, and other management techniques. Examples are Honokohau Ridge and upper valley (***above, right***) and Ukumehame Canyon (***left***).

Cameron Kepler

High in the mountains *mauka* (toward the mountains) of Lahaina sits a tiny, seldom-seen body of water, **VIOLET LAKE**. Mountain lakes are rare features on volcanic islands, and Maui is no exception. (*above*) A glorious panorama including Molokai; (*center*) typical weather at 4,960 feet. Here relatively pristine rain forests and high elevation bogs soak up copious rains with a sponge-like action, allowing for subterranean water storage. Receiving more than 400 inches of rainfall annually, this is one of the wettest spots on earth. Yet only six miles distant, the Lahaina-Kaanapali area, a natural semi-desert, receives less than 15 inches of annual rain. Although few people are aware of these natural forests, they are responsible for the lush landscaping in the resorts and residential areas.

(*bottom*) V-shaped **HONOKOWAI VALLEY**, with Violet Lake nestled near its upper reaches.

77

Maui Inter-Continental Wailea

(*left*) **PALAPALAI FERN** (*Microlepia strigosa*), which thrives at lower elevations, is a native fern most often seen in head-leis of hula dancers. One of the few native ferns used by early Hawaiians which is still worn by **DANCERS** today (*above*), *palapalai* serves to remind us how Hawaii's rich cultural traditions have for centuries been linked with the priceless bounty of land and sea.

(*left*) A particularly beautiful tract of **ISOLATED RAIN FOREST** is Hanaula, whose rugged topography is carpeted so extensively with ferns that it has earned the botanical distinction of being the "ferniest spot in Hawaii." Hanaula, now a Natural Area Reserve, harbors 65 of the state's 176 species of ferns. For comparison, there are approximately 100 fern species in the entire northeast and central regions of North America.

The tall, rosetted **PUE** (*Lobelia gaudichaudii*), with its long spikes of purple and white flowers, lives only in soggy bogs of the Hawaiian Islands.

(*left*) One of Hawaii's **NATIVE MINTS** (*Phyllostegia* sp.) blooms amid a tapestry of ferns, orchids and other delicate understory plants. The amount of habitat under which such floral gems flourish has been severely depleted over the years by unrestrained cattle. (*right*) OHA-WAI (*Clermontia oblongifolia*) lives near Puu Kukui, its only known location on Maui.

79

(*above*) Cerise flowers adorn the multi-branching **KOLII** (*Trematolobelia macrostachys*), a denizen of high elevation forest edge and bogs. There is no easy way to reach these forests; hikers may inquire with the Sierra Club or Mauna Ala hiking club for further information.

(*left*) This strange flowerhead with its huge scalloped leaves belongs to a member of a little-known family, Gunneraceae, whose few scattered members are in South America, New Zealand and Hawaii. It prefers the banks of steep gullies; each plant lives for decades, creeping slowly over water-soaked slopes. The Hawaiian name is **APEAPE** (*Gunnera petaloidea*).

(*right*) Another striking member of the mint family is *Stenogyne kamehamehae*, a **NATIVE VINE** which lacks both English and Hawaiian common names. Unique to Maui and Molokai this species exhibits much variation in leaf shape and flower color. Pictured is the cream-colored variety, less common than the pink form.

Cameron Kepler

(*above*) Shrouded in almost continual mists in high elevation bogs above 5,000 feet grows this small **EKE SILVERSWORD** (*Argyroxiphium calignis*), a two-foot-high cousin of the famous Haleakala silversword. Its entire world population covers only a few acres in West Maui, now part of the West Maui (Kahakuloa) Natural Area Reserve which is hunted and fenced to control pigs. Mt. Eke as seen from near Puu Kukui. This is one of the most pristine forested areas in Hawaii. Note Kahakuloa Heads in the far distance (*left*).

As the entire mass of West Maui is circular, if you hike inland via ridge or valley you quickly encounter precipitous, deeply-eroded terrain. This is why the Hawaiians still use the terms *mauka* (toward the mountains) and *makai* (toward the sea); they often make more sense than "north," "south," "east" or "west." The **NORTHERN VALLEYS** are incredibly beautiful and precipitous. The few maintained trails require permission and are best hiked through the Sierra or Mauna Ala hiking clubs, or the Boy Scouts. The upper sidewalls of Waihee Valley drop a dizzying 4,000 feet down to the narrow streambed below. In 1884, 105 years before this photograph was taken, the Reverend J. M. Alexander, after climbing this same ridge, commented: *"The almost incessant fogs of this region lift to give more than glimpses of the magnificent surrounding panorama...of the vast depths of Waihee clothed even over the most rocky precipices with enchanting vegetation...It is an extremely difficult task to ascend...but those who only travel the dusty highways near the shores of these islands know little of the enchanting scenery to be enjoyed by such a climb as this into the mountains of West Maui"* (*Hawaiian Almanac and Annual*, 1884).

David Boynton

John Carothers

The only tropical rain forests in the U.S. grow in the far-flung islands of Hawaii. Hawaii's native plants, which evolved over several million years, are so unique that 90% of them are not found anywhere else in the world! Feral **PIGS** (*above*), a combination of Polynesian and European breeds, have created such severe damage to the precious forests and watersheds of all Hawaii's islands that today millions of dollars are spent by state, federal and private agencies to hunt these vermin aggressively in order that Hawaii's fresh water supplies, tourist economy and agriculture may survive. (*center*) Fresh **PIG ROOTINGS** permanently destroy the delicate balance of mountaintop bogs. (*bottom*) A **ONCE-FORESTED SLOPE**, recovering after pig damage, is now strewn with alien grasses and rotting tree stumps. Note that present conservation problems in Hawaii are not all a direct result of man's activities.

83

V KAANAPALI

Centuries ago the coast and hills surrounding Kaanapali were clothed in native dryland and mesic forests—sacred *ohia* trees from which spiritual carvings were sculpted, *akia* shrubs which yielded fish poison and tough cordage, *wiliwili* trees from which small surfboards were fashioned, and *ilima*, whose tiny yellow flowers were strung into royal leis. Birdlife was abundant, including several species of flightless geese and ibises. Seabirds nested in vast colonies from shore to forest, while on the beaches green turtles dug nests and monk seals lazed around with their pups.

After the early Hawaiians moved in, the area grew in cultural and historical richness, but the precious *aina* (land) was not resilient after disturbance. Fires, in particular, resulted in a permanent loss of woodland cover and many plant species which were dependent upon shade for their survival. By the time the first explorers arrived in the late 18th century the land was *"so parched from its southern exposure to the powerful heat of the (sun's) rays…its scorched and shriveled produce of grass and herbage (was) incapable of any kind of cultivation"* (Menzies, *Journal of Vancouver's Voyage 1790-94*).

From the late 18th century, the history of West Maui is fairly well documented (also see Lahaina chapter). Like history anywhere, times were not always pleasant. Naturally, while this area was the focus of royal activities, a stock of myths and tales developed, some of which still survive. Hawaiians have always thrived on story-telling: in ancient times they were called *moolelo*, today one simply "talks story." Several stories center around Black Rock (see Sheraton Hotel) and the sleeping stone (see Maui Eldorado Condominium).

The names of three prominent Maui chiefs who made history here— Piilani, Kekaulike and Kahekili—are well-remembered today. Piilani and his son Kiha (15th century) left the most constructive impression, as they widened the ancient trail (*alaloa*) from Hana to Kaanapali, portions of which can still be seen today. Two highways (unjoined) around the southern flanks of Haleakala are still called Piilani Highway.

Kekaulike established a powerful kingdom on Maui which he ruled for over 50 years in the 18th century. During his reign Maui's people and lands became terribly impoverished, a legacy later documented by early Western explorers.

Kahekili, the last of Maui's traditional *alii* (royalty), also inherited the warrior spirit of his forebears. During his 25-year reign (late 18th century) Kahekili conquered all the major islands except Hawaii (Big Island), but today most of his bloody battles are forgotten, and he is remembered primarily for his daring

Kaanapali Beach Hotel

Dancers with kahili at a Lei Day (May 1) celebration.

leaps off Black Rock. His name is immortalized in Kahekili Highway, the coastal road which skirts West Maui's northern flanks (see last chapter).

In 1824 *kiawe* was introduced to Hawaii from Peru. Pre-adapted to semi-desert conditions, it spread into the dry West Maui foothills, creating vast unproductive stretches of spiny scrubland. Free-ranging, feral goats nibbled voraciously at every green shoot, finishing off most of the original vegetation. A few native plant species struggle to survive today, assisted by their Rare and Endangered status.

In the 1840s the slopes and lowlands around Kaanapali were converted into sugar fields, worked by imported Oriental laborers. Because sugar requires enormous amounts of water to be commercially productive (240 gallons per pound), almost all of West Maui's streams have been diverted for irrigation and no longer flow to the ocean. The area remained primarily agricultural until 1960.

Today it is difficult to visualize Kaanapali's former remoteness. When I first "journeyed" there from Kahului in the early '60s—an entire day's outing—the road was mostly dusty and unpaved. The upcoming Sheraton Hotel was front-page news and excited school children were taken on "field trips" there to witness such a colossal building!

From 1960-1990 immense changes occurred. The once isolated beaches and bays metamorphosed into a developer's (and tourist's) dream: 600 acres of landscaped hotels, condominiums, golf courses, roads, shops and restaurants. Kaanapali Beach Resort, opened in 1962 by AMFAC Corporation (American Factors), is now a coveted international vacation destination. Its name is easy to pronounce—"ka-ah-nah-pah-lee."

Every effort is made to delight the visitor. Acres of lush tropical vegetation, waterfalls, pools, fountains, glorious ocean views, first-rate art, varied entertainment, attractive waitresses, scrumptious food, babysitting services, and an orchid on every pillow...all are offered with an air of elegance in an Hawaiian setting. The very best aspects of Hawaiian traditions are presented, including crafts demonstrations and classes, music, dance, and appreciation of historical events and sacred sites. For business and conference delegates, multitudinous amenities such as notary services, Japanese translation and state-of-the-art office equipment are available. For sports enthusiasts, there are large tennis facilities and picturesque championship golf fairways that attract prestigious tournaments such as the Canada Cup and Women's Kemper Open. There are also wind-surfing, snorkeling, swimming, sailing, whale-watching, fitness rooms, discos, catamarans and three miles of wide, golden beaches for simply lazing around in the sun.

The Westin Maui

(*top*) **KAANAPALI'S SKYLINE** from offshore, bathed in rainbow-clad morning light, and from Kekaa Drive over the North Golf Course (*below*).

ART

In addition to their manicured gardens, decorated lobbies and stylish rooms, Kaanapali resorts feature paintings, sculptures, statues, chandeliers, and other quality *objets d'art*. The only way to appreciate each hotel's unique "gallery" setting is to experience it firsthand.

(*above*) These **THAI DANCERS** are part of the Hyatt's palatial art collection, whose value exceeds $2 million. Other treasures from Asia and the Pacific, artfully placed indoors and out, include Chinese cloisonne vases, etched mirrors, stone elephants, wooden animals and a golden Buddha.

(*below*) Clustered metal **KAHILI** stand tall at Kaanapali's first entrance. These familiar insignia of bygone days—colored cylinders originally adorned with feathers from native birds—are still indispensable on ceremonial occasions.

(*left*) At the Westin Maui and Hyatt Regency resorts the visitor is welcomed, indoors and out, by more than 2,000 **ART PIECES**: paintings, sculptures, murals, and vases. All carry an Asian flavor and are interwoven with fresh flowers against the living backdrop of Maui's beautiful seascape.

Reminiscent of international opulence, Kaanapali's deluxe hotels exude grandeur. This beautiful, uniquely-Pacific **SHELL CHANDELIER** sparkles in a promenade at the Hyatt Regency.

Maui's resort hotels are living art galleries for flower lovers. This exquisite **FLOWER ARRANGEMENT** presents heliconias (both upright and hanging), anthuriums and assorted tropical foliage in an harmonious blend of color and design. One stem of island-grown heliconias sells for as much as $35 in New York.

A docile **MACAW** cocks his head for petting (*above*), while a child feeds tame **SWANS** (*lower left*). Both the Westin and Hyatt have large collections of exotic birds— flamingos, parrots, and penguins—living "art" to complement the outdoor sculptures and waterscapes.

89

BEACHES, WATER SPORTS AND SNORKELING

The major hotels provide a variety of **PLEASURE CRAFT** for rent, charter or instruction: catamarans, yachts, Hobie Cats, lasers, windsurfing rigs, kayaks, and boogie boards. The Sheraton even advertises U.F.O.s (Unusual Floating Objects)! Snorkeling trips, winter whale-watching jaunts, and sunset cruises can be booked in resort lobbies. Sailing cruises (*opposite top*) also depart from Lahaina and Maalaea. Jet skis are discouraged in swimming areas.

Watching outrigger canoes is an exciting pastime. Canoe-racing is so popular in Hawaii that 63 canoe clubs (six on Maui) enjoy an international reputation. Check for regattas in local publications. Each fall, a 27.6-mile dash across a deep channel laced with tricky currents begins at Fleming Beach Park, Kapalua, and ends at Kaunakakai, Molokaï. Paddlers of all ages and diverse ethnic backgrounds participate. It's a grand social event and a chance to admire the beautifully crafted, wooden "Hawaiian racers." Canoes, up to 43 feet long are modeled after originals hewn from *koa* and other native woods. (*below*) **PARASAILING**, parachuting above a motor boat, is one of the numerous water sports available at Kaanapali. Maui's channels, though leeward of the West Maui Mountains, are not always as calm as this.

John Severson

Kaanapali Beach Hotel

Between Lahaina and Kaanapali are two beachside picnic areas popular with local families: **WAHIKULI STATE PARK** (pron. "wa-hee-coo-lee," *left*) and **HANAKAOO PARK** (pron. "hah-nah-ka-oh-oh," *right*). Both are safe for all types of water-oriented fun. You may even chance upon canoeing activities. From Hanakaoo you can walk along South Kaanapali Beach, over Black Rock, and along the north beach for up to three miles.

Kaanapali's irresistible **BEACHES**, three golden miles of them, need no introduction. Although wide and scenic, with summer temperatures averaging 77°F in the morning and 82°F in the afternoon, they slope unevenly underwater, so be careful. If the shorebreak is intimidating, keep away. Suspended coral debris can cut feet, causing infections.

Never turn your back on waves; even small breakers can knock adults head over heels. *Use sunscreen lotions*; Maui's sun is strong even in "winter." *Leave earrings, watches, wallets and other valuables in a safe place*, preferably away from the beach. Pictured are beaches at the Maui Marriott (**top**), Sheraton Maui (**center**), and Royal Lahaina (**below**). Public access to Kaanapali Beach is difficult because of limited parking. Concerned Maui residents are currently working to procure easier beach access for residents.

The Westin Maui

Portable watercraft for different age-groups create colorful views at Kaanapali: (*top*) A
WINDSURFING RIG affords a 360-degree panorama. Waters here are generally unsuitable
for regular surfing, but one of the world's best surfing bays lies only a few miles north.
(*bottom*) A tiny visitor from Japan delights in an oceanside pool.

93

SNORKELING—a journey into the underwater world—is a special experience that can be enjoyed by nearly everyone. Clear waters and relatively gentle swimming please novice and experienced snorkelers alike at Kaanapali. Black Rock is best. Here are a few pointers that will set your mind at ease and help to protect this fragile environment:

1. *Don't worry about sharks.* Hawaii's inshore waters are essentially free of dangerous sharks during the daytime. Dusk or night snorkeling is not recommended, as tiger sharks occasionally swim close to shore after dark.

2. *Don't poke your fingers into, or enter, holes or caves.* Hawaii has several species of moray eels and lobsters that hurt people. Leave cave exploration to those with experience.

3. *Don't touch sea urchins,* especially the big black ones with long, skinny spines. Stings from their needles are painful.

4. *Don't walk or even rest your feet on the coral reef or on rocks covered with marine life.* Marine invertebrate animals (especially corals) are fragile and easily crushed.

5. *Don't venture into surge channels or crevices when the sea is rough.* The sea is powerful, and even small waves can bash your body against rocks, causing scrapes and cuts. Grazed skin from coral cuts is particularly painful and prone to infection.

Snorkeling gear can be rented at all resorts. Prescription masks and underwater cameras may be available. (**left**)

(**above left**) The **UNICORN TANG** (*Naso unicornis*) is usually seen in small schools. Its blue coloration and short central snout, whose function is unknown, are identifying characteristics. (**above right**) **FOURSPOT BUTTERFLYFISH** (*Chaetodon quadrimaculatus*) poke under a ledge encrusted with red sponges (*Microciona* sp.) (**above**) A school of **CONVICT TANG** or *manini* (*Acanthurus sandvicensis*).

Ed Robinson

An unusual, skinny reef fish, widespread geographically, is the **CHINESE TRUMPET FISH** (*Aulostoma chinensis*, or *nunu*). The round-bodied, yellow reef fish in this photo include lemon butterflyfish (*Chaetodon miliaris*), raccoon butterflyfish (*Chaetodon lunula*) and fourspot butterflyfish. In past times, fish such as these were caught abundantly in circular thrownets.

Ed Robinson

Foraging in different areas of the coralheads are three **COMMON REEF-FISH: (*left to right*)** large blue parrot fish (*Scarus perspicillatus*), Moorish idol (*Zanclus cornutus*), and yellow-tail wrasse (*Coris gaimardi*). The last species sometimes buries itself in the bottom sand when resting.

During winter, Kaanapali's main thoroughfare bursts alive when leafless branches bear clusters of fiery **TIGER'S CLAWS** (*Erythrina* species). Listen for the high-pitched twittering of the **JAPANESE WHITE-EYE** (*Zosterops japonicus*), a tiny green bird with prominent white eye-rings.

Robert Shallenberger

(**left**) **MYNAH BIRDS** (*Acridotheres tristis*), noisy brown birds ubiquitous in all Hawaii's lowlands, were originally introduced from India to control insect pests in sugarcane fields.
(**right**) **ZEBRA DOVES** (*Geopelia striata*), one of Hawaii's common lowland birds, may be seen along roadsides, on lawns and in gardens busily pecking for seeds. Almost all familiar birds in the islands have been introduced from other tropical countries. Native birds, many of which are endangered, are restricted to mountain forests above 3,000 feet elevation.

DINING

Hyatt Regency Maui

The Westin Maui

The Westin Maui

EXOTIC COCKTAILS lure travelers. Often accompanied by specialty *hors d'oeuvres*, the choices include pina coladas, mai tais, rum and champagne punches, tropical fruit smoothies, etc. Each is presented as a colorful work of liquid art.

Kaanapali's restaurants are internationally renowned. Food, impeccably fresh and excellently prepared, includes Continental, American, Polynesian, Oriental and seafood cuisine and, naturally, a bounty of island dishes. This delicious abundance is served from dawn till midnight at poolside cafs, coffee shops, sunset cruise diners, pizza parlors, sinful(!) dessert shops, "happy hour" bars, gourmet restaurants, and lavish Sunday brunches. The Royal Lahaina Resort even offers a "grazing restaurant," which features a sumptuous variety of oriental *hors d'oeuvres*. Eat in your bathing suit or in a glittering gown. Pictured are the Hyatt's **SWAN COURT (left)** and the Westin's **SOUND OF THE FALLS (right)**, two sophisticated restaurants, each overlooking its own pool. The latter offers a regal blend of French and Japanese culinary styles.

*For conventions, receptions and theme party diners, huge banquet rooms
are decked out in splendor.*

Shady and outdoorsy, poolside cafés and bars offer culinary delights in a casual setting, often with gentle Hawaiian music. Room service and minibars with fruit juices, sodas, standard drinks and snacks are standard. The following is a small selection of excellent eateries (*center left*): "Cook's at the Beach," Maui Westin; (*center right*) "Moana Terrace," Maui Marriott; (*bottom*) balcony, Sheraton Maui; (*top right*) the **TIKI TERRACE** bar, Kaanapali Beach Hotel, is presided over by a benign *tiki* (Polynesian good luck symbol).

Maui Marriott

Several resorts offer nightly **LUAUS**, the delectable Hawaiian banquets of staple foods and delicacies gathered from centuries of intermingling peoples: ancient Polynesians, Chinese, Japanese, Filipinos, Americans and the multiethnic residents of contemporary Hawaii. The *piece de resistance* is *kalua* pig, a whole pig steamed in an underground oven (*imu*) then shredded in the traditional Polynesian manner. Savor its delicate smokiness and unusual texture. Sample the *haupia* (coconut pudding), *poi* (gummy, pounded taro—dip morsels of meat into it), fresh fruit and fancy desserts, epicurean luxury beyond the wildest dreams of the ancient Hawaiians. After eating, sit back and enjoy the Polynesian show. (**bottom**) Pictured is a beachside *luau* at the Sheraton Maui.

For true extravagance, **INTERNATIONAL** or **HAWAIIAN BUFFETS**, specialties of all the resorts, are unbeatable. Dozens (hundreds?) of scrumptious *hors d'oeuvres* (pupus), entrees, fruits, breads, and desserts can satisfy the hungriest guest. (**left**) Royal Lahaina Resort. (**right**) Sheraton Maui.

Royal Lahaina Resort/Evan Mower

Sheraton Maui

ENTERTAINMENT

No book on Hawaii would be complete without a **HULA DANCER** . Evolving over centuries, this graceful dance, where hand movements tell a story, may today be admired in myriad forms—from "ancient hula" (*kahiko*) danced in 19th century costumes with *ti*-leaf skirts and head leis, to "modern hula," danced in long muumuus. Nightly entertainment and special weekly shows are well advertised, as are annual festivals such as "Na Mele O Maui" (November) and Kamehameha Day (June). Sponsored by the Kaanapali Beach Operators Association, these popular cultural events perpetuate Hawaiian traditions of dancing, chanting and singing.

Hyatt Regency Maui

Steve Read

(**right**) To be charmed by a cute little dancing girl in a flowery muumuu, be sure to attend "Na Mele."

(**bottom left**) Two **KAMAAINA DANCERS** glow after a performance.

Steve Read

Tahitian dancers are always a favorite at Kaanapali.

HAWAIIAN MUSIC abounds in Kaanapali. *(below)* A statewide event that also includes elaborate festivities and floral extravaganzas is **LEI DAY** (May 1). Leis adorn dancers and many citizens. Public schools prepare weeks ahead for class presentations of dancing, free to all. Consult the telephone book for a State Cultural Calendar. The Kaanapali Beach Hotel directs its own hula school (halau), attended free of charge by children of employees. Pictured *(below)* is the Employees' Lei Day Court, featuring costumes, cloth kahili, and leis of maile and seashells.

Kaanapali Beach Hotel/Maui Custom Color

Kaanapali Beach Hotel/Maui Custom Color

Kaanapali Beach Hotel

LEI-MAKING, ukelele playing, *lauhala* weaving, *lavalava* (sarong) wrapping, *ti*-leaf hula skirt weaving, Hawaiian quilting, hula lessons and local food preparation are among the light cultural entertainments which provide educational fun for guests of all ages.

Skinner Communications

The **MAUI SYMPHONY ORCHESTRA** presents its annual July 4 concert on the Kaanapali golf course, accompanied by appropriate aerial celebrations.

Mike Horikawa/Hyatt Regency Maui

Fire-dancing, the twisting and juggling of single- and double-ended flaming rods, is an astonishing acrobatic feat.

Kaanapali is abundantly and beautifully landscaped. (For more flowers see the Lahaina chapter.)

HAWAII'S STATE FLOWER (*Hibiscus* species and hybrids), perks up roadsides, parking lots and the well-maintained gardens of Kaanapali, adding splashes of year-round color. Pick one and tuck it behind your ear (right ear if "available," left one if "taken"). The smaller flowers **(right)** last only one day; the larger hybrids **(lower right)** last two days.

Glorious billowy masses of **RAINBOW SHOWER TREES** (*Cassia x nealiae*) color summer landscaping.

A lubiquitos landscapping ornamental is the **OCTOPUS TREE** (*Brassaia actinophylla*), whose long floral arms mimic those of its marine namesake. Even when not blooming, this Australian curiosity is easily recognizee by its umbrella-shaped, radially divided leaves. A popular house plant the world over, you may have a miniature version in your living room of office.

The huge parasols of dazzling scarlet blossoms and lacy foliage sprinkled liberally around Kaanapali are **ROYAL POINCIANAS** (*Delonix regia*).

A newcomer to Hawaii's landscaping, sexy pink heliconia (Heliconia chartacea cv. 'Sexy Pink') bespeaks tropical beauty.

The Westin Maui

(*top*) The verdant **FAIRWAYS** of the Royal Kaanapali Golf Courses (North and South), the first visitor-oriented golf courses built in Hawaii, occupy former wetland taro (a starchy vegetable) and horse-racing land. All hotels and condos provide shuttle service to the clubhouse and pro shop.

Royal Lahaina Resort

Extensive **GOLF COURSES** add green space to the resort complex. Annual golf tournaments, parades, cultural festivals and July the Fourth celebrations are held within its 600-acre confines. Photos show the North Course looking toward the Royal Lahaina (*center*) and across sand traps to the Sheraton Maui (*below*). Since its opening in 1962, the North Course has hosted the World Cup, International Golf Championship, and the Women's Kemper Open. Legend relates that in the area between the third and fourth tees of the North Course was a cave called *Ke Ana Pueo*, the Owl Cave. A guardian spirit dwelling here often helped people by appearing in her owl form and counseling them wisely.

Royal Lahaina Resort

The Royal Lahaina Tennis Ranch and Stadium, a statewide mecca for **TENNIS** buffs, offer excellent facilities and free shuttle service all over Kaanapali. It is also open to the public. Annual tournaments, including the Royal Lahaina Open and Hawaii High School State Tournament, use its 2,500-seat stadium, the largest in Hawaii. You might even chance upon your favorite player scooping up a trophy! Facilities include 11 plexipave courts (six lit at night), ball machines, pool, Jacuzzi, locker rooms, massage therapists, pro shop, player match-up and racquet-stringing services, wheelchair tennis, and lessons for all ages—in Japanese if you like!

Skinner Communications/Maui Marriott

A shaded beachside **SHUFFLEBOARD** court (*left*) at the Sheraton is fun for an easy change of pace. If the pressures of job, family and social obligations have sapped your energy, let Maui's healing atmosphere restore you with a little pampering (*right*).

The Hyatt Regency Hotel is a lavish, 18-acre, $80 million resort and scenic attraction, complete with a mini-zoo, a two-mile network of streams and waterfalls weaving through pools and gardens, an outstanding open-air Asian-Pacific art exhibit, a "swan lake," disco, swim-up cocktail bar, special rooms for the handicapped, international shopping, theme parties, a 70-foot-high banyan tree in an indoor "atrium," and the usual plethora of recreational activities and visitor services. It has 815 guestrooms and suites.

The Hyatt, which opened in 1980, fronts the most southerly portion of Kaanapali Beach. Here lies the only offshore snorkeling reef on the three-mile beach, visible in the aerial photo below. Note that the beach rises steeply from the water's edge. **(below)** **AERIAL VIEW** of south Kaanapali, showing the Hyatt Regency, golden beaches and the West Maui Mountains.

The hotel's focal point is an unusual **TRIPARTITE POOL**, whose $1 million worth of artificial rocks, molded from fiberglass and concrete, were patterned after boulders in the Sierra Nevada Mountains of California. This artistic rock system (natural as well as simulated) totals 37,000 square feet, providing the formerly flat terrain some "mini-topography." Interwoven with these rocks are Japanese and tropical gardens housing an outstanding, Asian-Pacific art "museum." Each *objet d'art* can be enjoyed, alone, in its own landscaped setting (see also The Westin Maui).

An enticing **GROTTO** bisects the half-acre pool. From the blue, wavy-edged Lahaina pool you can swim through a waterfall, pass into a cavern, then duck under a second waterfall by the Napili lagoon. See if you can find the secret cave.

This Napili section of the pool, with its tiled bottom and lush plantings, resembles a greenish **LAGOON**. It may be entered by swimming under a waterfall from the grotto, diving from the side, or splashing in from the end of a twisting, 130-foot-long slide. Non-swimmers can watch water activities from a rickety swinging bridge. (Hang on!) The entire scene seems lifted from the pages of a storybook.

SUNBATHING to the restful sounds of water.

MAUI MARRIOTT

Among the distinctions of this deluxe resort is its 1984 award as one of the "10 Best Resorts for Meetings" in the nation. Located on 15 oceanfront acres of Kaanapali Beach, its ample outdoor space is matched by its large rooms containing state-of-the-art luxuries such as cable movies on the TV, direct-dial phone, and minibar. Each room is decorated with a lithograph by the renowned artist Pegge Hopper, who specializes in painting Hawaiian people. In addition to the usual prodigious array of recreational and service amenities, the Marriott has a nine-hole putting green, a video game room, and secretarial, telex, facsimile and notary service.

Dining specialties include Maui's first *teppan-yaki* restaurant, the Nikko Japanese Steak House where trained chefs grill foods and dazzle guests with nimble knife-wielding, right at their table.

As with the other portions of Kaanapali Beach, swimming conditions are idyllic in all but periods of high surf. At such times water pounds on the beach and strong rip tides are generated. Sit high up on the grass and enjoy (though vicariously) the thrills of surfers riding the powerful swells.

Maui Marriott

A replica of an authentic **HAWAIIAN THATCHED HUT**, complete with *koa* canoe, stands on the beautifully landscaped grounds. Note the absence of windows as Hawaiians lived primarily outdoors. All hotels offer educational courses in hula and Hawaiian crafts.

A curvaceous **FREE-FORM POOL** at the Maui Marriott incorporates cascades, a window to the ocean, and shady tropical plantings.

The **MARRIOTT'S FOUR-STORY LOBBY**, connecting its two nine-story, 720-room guest wings, is planted with a sumptuous array of tropical vegetation surrounding pools, fountains and an outrigger canoe.

FOUNTAINS, a Marriott specialty, squirt, spray, and trickle almost everywhere you look. This giant clam shell (**top**) adorns the lobby, while the spouting "crown" (**bottom**) sparkles beside an outdoor café.

113

THE WESTIN MAUI

The Westin Maui is an exemplary resort packed with fun, art, sports, Hawaiiana, a mini-zoo, waterfalls, and pools. Designed by Chris Hemmeter, who also created the neighboring Hyatt Regency, it offers its numerous amenities, sparkling cleanliness, and precise attention to detail.

The Westin's entire color scheme—shades of muted pinks with complementary blues, mauves and neutral tones—is so pleasingly coordinated it appears that a single artist has hand-picked every flagstone, quilt, and carpet. A $155 million remake of the old Maui Surf Hotel, the Westin Maui blends beauty of the past with state-of-the-art technology. The Westin provides guests with an excellent user's manual for the ocean.

The Westin Maui

The Westin Maui

The Westin's **CURVACEOUS ARCHITECTURE** of coral and beige, designed to maximize ocean views, encloses 12 acres of an Asian-Pacific "wonderland."

The **FRONT LOBBY** wafts you into an exotic tropical world which simultaneously stimulates and soothes the senses. Enjoy impeccable surroundings and excellent food amid gently cascading water and plumeria-scented air.

114

Swish down the sleekly snaky course of this 150-foot **WATERSLIDE** into the Maui Pool (*left*). Don't worry about injuring your back—the slide has rubberized cushioning. A gentler, 20-foot chute (*below*) entertains youngsters.

The Westin Maui

Focused around a dazzling aquatic playground, the Westin boasts 55,000 sq. ft. of amoeboid-shaped pools and interconnecting waterways, and 25,000 sq. ft. of deck space.
WATERFALLS range from formal "bridal veils" (*left*) to intimate, palm-fringed falls (*right*) which ruffle waterfowl reflections or bounce playfully off swimmers. A tunneled cave with peek-holes open to the sky and views of tumbling waterfalls (undoubtedly inspired by Hawaii's natural coastlines and lava tubes) features a swim-and-clamber-up Jacuzzi.

KAANAPALI BEACH HOTEL

Kaanapali Beach Hotel

Kaanapali Beach Hotel, relatively small (431 rooms), offers most of the luxuries and privileges of the larger resorts, and shares similar panoramas. Hawaiian *aloha* is such an important concept here that the management holds regular classes to enhance the employees' appreciation of island culture and values, which in turn are passed on to visitors. Their Project *Pookela*, the State's only "hotel school," teaches Hawaiian language, geography, religion, mythology, ethnobotany (traditional uses of plants), economics and technology.

Enjoy the gracious *aloha* of this "very Hawaiian hotel." A unique fountain in the form of an **ERUPTING VOLCANO** spews water by day (**below**) and red "lava" by night (**top**). Adjacent to Whaler's Village Shopping Center, this "homey" hotel even provides specialty recipe cards on request.

(*top*) A **WHALE-SHAPED POOL** and nearby 40 sq. ft. giant checkerboard decorate the grounds.

(*left*) Resplendent in forest sunshine, the maple-like **KUKUI** (*Aleurites moluccana*), a Polynesian tree which formerly provided "candles" and which also represents enlightenment, has recently been adopted into the hotel logo.

Interest in Hawaiian culture includes native and Polynesian-introduced plants. Pictured is the extremely rare **OHAI** (pron. "oh-hi," *left*), *Sesbania tomentosa*. The beachfront gardens (**right**) ramble spaciously; some trees are labeled.

117

SHERATON MAUI

Sheraton Maui

In 1963 the Sheraton Maui's opening made history—as the first hotel built by a major corporation outside Waikiki. It was also the first hotel at Kaanapali (see also Royal Lahaina) and the first planned vacation resort in Hawaii. The Sheraton also developed the first "hanging gardens," circular lanais (porches), and elevators on Maui and was responsible for the islands' first commercial jet landing. So novel was this event that schools closed, people cheered visitor buses, and storefronts proclaimed "Sheraton Maui Week."

The resort occupies a choice position centered on Black Rock, a site of great religious significance to ancient Hawaiians. According to tradition, Black Rock was a *leina a ka uhane* or "soul's leap," where, at the moment of physical death, the body's life force was transported elsewhere by a minor deity.

Sheraton Maui

The Sheraton's original layout earned it the nickname "upside-down hotel": you walked into the clifftop lobby then rode the elevator *down* to the rooms and pool. Today the lobby is at street level, but on the clifftop, **AIRY BALCONIES**, restaurants and shops still enjoy a fabulous panorama and the hotel's spacious 26-acre grounds. Visit the prow of an Hawaiian war canoe, focal point for a fountain, and read the legend inscribed there. Notice the tiny pool in which floating flowers daily inscribe a Sheraton "S."

118

The ancients named **BLACK ROCK** *Puu Kekaa* ("hill creating strength through enlightenment"). They held daily gatherings to thank La, the Sun, for the gifts of light and all things good. On this rocky promontory prayers were also offered to all departed souls who had sprung from earth to the nether land. In a lighter vein, Black Rock was Chief Kahekili's favorite **CLIFF-JUMPING** spot. The chief was especially revered for his courage to have fun at a religious site.

In 1963 the Sheraton started several Kaanapali **TRADITIONS**. Every night a *malo* (loincloth)-clad youth throws a lei into the sea, blows a conch shell, lights the evening torches, then dives off Black Rock. You too can perform daredevil feats like the royalty of old—these days people jump or dive off its snaggy lava every day. Such frivolity evidently does not concern the gods any longer.

Douglas Peebles

Kaanapali Beach Association

The word Kaanapali is translated as "rolling cliffs" or "division-cliff," an astute name for this long stretch of beach halved by Black Rock's crab-shaped promontory. The Sheraton Maui incorporates Black Rock into its very heart. Two six-story **TOWERS** hug the 80-foot-high cliff (*above*), while 26 Polynesian-style **COTTAGES** skirt its base (*lower right*).

ROYAL LAHAINA RESORT

The first hotel north of Black Rock, the Royal Lahaina Resort opened as a private club in 1962. The resort prides itself on its many time-honored employees, genuine Hawaiian hospitality, scrumptious eateries, and grounds replete with mature trees and immaculate lawns. The major tennis facilities, utilized by many hotels and condominiums, are housed here. It is proud to host faithful guests; long-time hotel babysitters have watched their children grow, and maids still remember personal details such as who prefers extra large pillows.

As is typical of five-star accommodations, a wide variety of rooms are available: standard, superior, deluxe, suites and cottages (some with full kitchens). The Royal Suite tops them off—a beachside cottage with private garden *and* pool!

Plush Oriental carpeting, elegant brocade wallpaper, floor-to-ceiling windows, Hawaiian motifs, audio-visual facilities, and creative lighting contribute to the appeal of the resort's 15,000 sq. ft. of ballrooms and conference rooms, esteemed for conventions of every type.

Viewed from above, its spreading 26 acres can be seen to flank a half-mile of golden, relatively unpopulated beach. The many open areas, providing agreeable shade during the midday heat, are used extensively for night parties. This resort is reputed for its elaborate theme parties, which include *Paniolo* (Hawaiian cowboy), M.A.S.H., and Pacific Nights, featuring 19th century Lahaina and Oriental scenes.

Royal Lahaina Resort

Charming **COTTAGES**, 22 in all, nestle amongst spacious mature landscaping. The brilliant crimson tree is royal poinciana (*Delonix regia*), flowering in summer.
(**left**) The **GAZEBO LAWN**, intimate and secluded, is perfect for weddings and small receptions.
(**below**) The nightly beachside luau, with *kalua* pig, lavish buffet, open bar, and costumed Polynesian dancers, is a time-honored tradition. The **FIRE KNIFE DANCE** is especially spectacular.

Royal Lahaina Resort/Evan Mower

121

CONDOMINIUMS

The condominium is a modern version of a rental house. The living space may be temporary or relatively permanent, a simple studio within a multistoried complex, or an elaborate home in a duplex. Condominiums are usually not set up by a single owner or corporation, but by a limited partnership of investors who possess proprietary rights to one or more units. All owners share in the maintenance and landscaping costs of the complex; thus all common areas are held jointly.

The visitor rents a living unit from management just as he or she would rent a hotel room. Condos are particularly favored by groups or families, as they are complete apartments having a variable number of bedrooms and bathrooms. Cooking facilities include every conceivable option from a basic refrigerator and stove to the all-American dream kitchen sporting a dishwasher, microwave, grill, wet bar, icemaker and coffeemaker, garbage disposal and telephone.

Hawaii has the largest number of condo units per capita in the nation, and Maui is second to Oahu for the state. In Kaanapali, they all tend to be fancy, and expensive to very expensive (Kihei, in South Maui, offers a wider price range for the budget-conscious). Rates are highest during Maui's peak season (mid-December to mid-April), for larger units and for ocean views.

Amenities include adult and children's swimming pools, air conditioning, golf and putting greens, weight-lifting and recreation rooms, sauna/Jacuzzis, barbecues, shuffleboard, tennis, private washing machines and dryers, daily maid service, toll-free phone service to the mainland, and so on. Some house restaurants and small grocery stores. Special services (on request) include complimentary airport pickup and return, rental car, starter grocery package, and guest-signing privileges at certain restaurants. Resort managements offer personally tailored Most condos are available through the Kaanapali Beach Operators' Association (808-661-3271). Due to limited space, only a few are treated briefly in this book.

The Whaler.

Kaanapali Royal.

(*clockwise*) Kaanapali Shores, Maui Eldorado, Kaanapali Alii, Maui Kaanapali Villas. All are located either on the beach or beside golf courses, with access to sports facilities including tennis. Close to the Maui Eldorado lies the *pohaku moemoe* or "sleeping stone," where the demigod Maui is said to have left his drowsy friend, Moemoe, to rest forever.

Aston Resorts

An isolated haven of elegance and beauty, the Kapalua Bay Hotel (*below*) fronts a superb shoreline that includes a secluded golden beach and rugged rocky promontories. The Hawaiian meaning of Kapalua, "arms embracing the sea," seems especially appropriate when the area is viewed from the air. The hotel's two arms of villas sloping toward the coast mirror this embrace. Kapalua enjoys refreshing breezes and a cooler atmosphere than does Lahaina, a result of trade winds wrapping around the north end of West Maui.

Surrounding this 750-acre, world-class resort complex are 23,000 acres of pineapple plantations owned by Maui Land and Pineapple Company, the resort's original planners and proprietors. In addition to the usual array of amenities, sports, food and entertainment, Kapalua also houses a magnificent collection of paintings by Hawaii artists.

Since the opening of the West Maui airfield in 1987, it has been possible to fly directly to Maui's west-side resorts in small aircraft (not jets). Rental cars are available but some condos and hotels offer free shuttle service to and from the airport.

Dripping with natural sweetness, **PINEAPPLES** are best picked when ripe. If picked green then airfreighted to the mainland, they turn yellow but never attain the delectable taste of natural sun-ripened fruit because the fruit's starches do not mature into sweet sugars after picking. A stable and profitable business of Maui, pineapple sales exceeded $45 million in 1986. It is an easy crop to replant: at the cannery, hundreds of spiny pineapple tops are twisted off, tossed into a pickup truck and returned immediately to the fields to be replanted. Each individual produces from two to five commercially useable fruits over a three-to-four-year growing cycle.

Harrington Photography/Kapalua Bay Hotel

The **KAPALUA BAY COURSE**, a 6,831-yard layout, commands stunning views of Molokai and the Pacific Ocean. Each November, one of the nation's premier golf events, the Isuzu Kapalua International, occurs here. This week-long festival attracts dozens of the world's finest professional golfers and receives both national and international television coverage. Proceeds are donated to Kahului's J. Walter Cameron Center which houses more than 20 charitable organizations.

Kapalua Bay Hotel

(left) KAPALUA BAY HOTEL, its elegant bowers entwined in tropical vegetation, blends contemporary and Mediterranean architectural motifs in a uniquely Hawaiian manner. The complex includes exclusive condominiums and residences and sponsors exhibitions by Maui artists.

(right) The resort, providing similar luxuries and amenities available to those at Kaanapali, exudes an aristocratic individuality that is enhanced by its isolated location and intimate crescentic **BEACH**. This beach is said to be the safest swimming beach on West Maui, even in winter.

Kapalua Bay Hotel

IMG Artists, New York

Another internationally-renowned event is the annual **KAPALUA MUSIC FESTIVAL**, a summer gathering for a select group of classical musicians. This two-week, informal musical extravaganza, taking place in an acoustically designed ballroom adorned with flowers, features a wealth of chamber music from Baroque to contemporary periods. Every year, a different combination of instruments is represented, always including a few of Hawaii's top **MUSICIANS** from the Honolulu Symphony. The festival was originally sponsored by the Cameron family, kamaainas who have been intimately involved with the development of arts, community and cultural affairs on Maui for more than 30 years and whose roots extend back five generations to early missionaries. The festival directors, Yizhak Schotten and Katherine Collier, now cooperate with the Maui Philharmonic Society.

Clarinetist **DAVID SHIFRIN** (*above*) and harpist **EMILY MITCHELL** (*below*) rank among the celebrated artists whose flawless technique, impeccable intonation and exceptional tone quality thrill numerous music lovers each year.

127

From Kapalua to a few miles past Nakalele, the road deteriorates progressively. Turn back before Kahakuloa as rental cars are prohibited from driving the rough track from Nakalele to Wailuku. Here the coastline changes character: beaches are fewer and less accessible. Lava cliffs rise steeply and wild waters boil along the shoreline. Houses are few, and the nearest gas station is many miles back in Lahaina. North of Kaanapali, the **CONDO-LINED BEACHES** (*left*) stretch through Honokowai and Kahana to Honokahua, then become increasingly rocky.

HONOLUA BAY, three miles past Kapalua, is one of the prime surfing breaks in the world. Although the bay encloses a relatively small area, its waves, generated from winter swells focusing into a narrow bay, are considered perfect. When the surf is "happening," you can sit atop the cliffs and admire Honolua's shapely, curling mounds of water energy as they roll gracefully towards shore. What an exquisite pale turquoise color at the apex of the wave just as it begins to break! The most proficient riders at Honolua may well be your favorite stars from *Surfer* magazine (pictured is Maui boy Brad Lewis). This bay was once the headquarters of Honolua Ranch, active from 1892-1914 when the first pineapples were planted.

Douglas Peebles

Cameron Kepler

HONOLUA BAY on a calm day. It is an underwater refuge, fine for summertime snorkeling, but don't venture out in winter unless you've had experience in rough seas.

ROCKY LAVA and rough waters characterize this section of coastline. The road is now moving onto the north shore, typified by trade winds and a wetter climate. At Nakalele Point, 18 miles north of Lahaina on Route 30, a Jeep trail leads to a bluff overlooking a Coast Guard beacon, a blowhole and extensive tidepool ledges. With suitable footwear (at least tennis shoes), the entire family can enjoy hiking around, rock-jumping and examining lava formations. Be careful. You're on your own here.

(*top*) West Maui's most prominent coastal feature is Kahakuloa Head, the "tall lord," a volcanic dome as tall as a 60-story building. Once referred to as "Maui's Gibraltar," **KAHAKULOA** stands guard over a tiny village of the same name, so rural it only received electricity in the 1950s.

(*right*) The **TIP OF WEST MAUI**, showing Kahakuloa (*left*) and Honokohau valleys (*right*) is one of the first sights that millions of people see when flying to Maui. Some say that Maui's nickname, "Valley Isle," refers to the island's numerous, deeply carved valleys characteristic of West Maui's mountains. Others say that the wide valley (actually an isthmus) between Haleakala and West Maui prompted the name. Take your choice.

Cameron Kepler

Cameron Kepler

(**above**) The noble profiles of two striking monoliths, **KAHAKULOA HEAD** (545 feet) and **PUU KAHULIANAPA** (545 feet) are seen in dawn light from Moke-ehia, a nearby island. Nestled within their steep bluffs a few extremely rare native plants may be found.

(**center**) A canoeist's view of Kahakuloa Heads as they peep through the gap separating Hakuhee Point and Moke-ehia Island.

(**bottom**) A landward view of the same, this time from Lanilili Peak (2,563 feet), a high cone on a ridge that soars beside dizzying precipices.

VI NORTH COAST AND VALLEYS

To drive around West Maui's wet north coast you must turn around, return to Wailuku on Route 30 and start afresh on Routes 33 and 34 (340). The first interesting spot, apart from macadamia nut orchards, is the Halekii-Pihana Heiaus State Monument off Waiehu Beach Road, Route 34. Here repose the remains of two *heiau* (places of worship) that were converted to war temples by Maui's last ruling chief, Kahekili.

The highways promise easy travel as you pass through the tiny sugar plantation towns of Waiehu and Waihee, after which the road disintegrates rapidly, becoming a twisty, dusty, pitted, clifftop route which resembles the "old Hana Highway." If you lived in Waihee a few decades ago, a village bell, now housed at the Maui Historical Society in Wailuku, would have awakened you daily at 4:30 a.m. Today, this small town houses many Filipinos, Maui's most recent immigrant group. Annual Filipino events include the "Miss Maui Filipina" pageant and ethnic dances in which beautiful girls, mostly tiny and slender, dress in traditional "butterfly-sleeved" costumes and dance to joyous folk music.

West Maui's rocky Northern Coastline is devoid of beaches, but its indented seacliffs (up to 450 feet high), offshore islands and natural grandeur make it unique in the islands. Kaemi Island and Makawana Point are pictured, showing distant Kahului Harbor.

A clump of wild taro adds a Polynesian touch to this canyon hidden within West Maui's labyrinthine recesses. Plunging to depths up to 3,000 feet, such cliffs rarely receive direct sunlight.

(*top*) The hiking clubs lead several **HIKES** in the lowland valleys of this coastline. Pictured is a swing bridge across the lower Waihee Valley. Further upstream you can walk beside irrigation ditches and marvel at the amount of hand labor wrought by chinese workers decades ago. (*below*) Battered by salty waves and "eaten away" by animals such as limpets (*opihi*) and sea urchins (*wana*), the two types of **LAVA** pictured here, pale chalky and dark basaltic, undergo continuous erosion into pitted fretwork and angular shapes reminiscent of contemporary art. Watch for **IWA** (Great Frigatebirds, *Fregata minor*) and **NOIO** (Common Noddies, *Anous stolidus*) along this coast (***center and bottom left respectively***). Spotting seabirds is always a pleasure.

Cameron Kepler

Cameron Kepler

Although the protea family is renowned for its striking flowers, one of its aberrant members, the **MACADAMIA NUT TREE** (*Macadamia ternifolia*), is famous for its delicious, fine-textured (and expensive!) nuts. On Maui, Wailuku Agribusiness (formerly Wailuku Sugar Company) has converted much of its land to macadamias. Growing in grape-like clusters among dark, prickly leaves, these extremely hard-shelled nuts take seven months to mature. After harvesting (September to November), the nut is cracked open and its "meat" fried briefly in coconut oil to enhance taste and texture.

Cameron Kepler

(*below*) **WATER EROSION AND VOLCANICITY**. One needs little imagination to relive these tremendous forces of nature here, where cascade-worn buttresses fall steeply into Waihee Valley. Haleakala's 10,000-foot volcanic mound forms an impressive backdrop to this hiker's view of West, Central and East Maui from 2,000 feet elevation.

John Carothers

135

HANA HIGHWAY

The scenic journey from Kaanapali along Maui's northeast and east coasts to Hana and Kipahulu, can mean a very long day: one hour to Kahului, two (plus) hours to Hana, and one hour to Kipahulu. As rental cars are not permitted on the rough southern route, you must return the same way you came, making this a journey of seven to eight hours' driving.

This twisting, narrow mountain road cannot be whizzed around hastily. Stop frequently and absorb all of its expansive views, colors, smells, and sounds. Even if you never reach Hana the trip will be most rewarding.

Audio-visual treats along this 52-mile, 617-curve, and 56-bridge "highway" include lush rain forests, wave-thrashed shores, dizzying precipices, spectacular waterfalls, freshwater caves, tropical arboretae, historic churches, sacred temple sites and burial grounds, and the grave of Charles Lindbergh.

Remember to fill up with gasoline in Paia, take food and drink (streamwater is unhealthy), grab your raincoat, and don't fall over the cliffs! For mile-by-mile pictorial details, see *Maui's Hana Highway: A Visitor's Guide*, by A. K. Kepler (Mutual Publishing).

Renowned surfing beach, Hookipa.

The lushly verdant Hana Highway.

Cameron Kepler

Kaumahina cliffs and Keanae Peninsula.

Taro, destined for the *poi* factory, Keanae.

Hana Highway at Honomanu Bay.

Crashing surf at dusk, Keanae.

Waianapanapa State Park.

Alau Island, Hana.

Oheo Gulch (Seven Pools), Kipahulu.

Makahiku Falls, Kipahulu.

Cameron Kepler

Cameron Kepler

Cameron Kepler

SOUTH MAUI—KIHEI, WAILEA, MAKENA

An easy coastal drive, south of Maalaea, features a 12-mile stretch of sweeping golden beaches and intimate coves (Maui's "Gold Coast"), expansive views of the West Maui Mountains and four nearby islands, and a wildlife refuge. Kihei specializes in condominiums, while the Wailea-Makena area, with its immaculate landscaping and tropical opulence, is the southern equivalent of Kaanapali. Crescentic Molokini Island, popular for snorkeling, provides grand views of nearby islands, including Kahoolawe, and the opportunity to spot whales, dolphins, and seabirds.

South Maui can be covered in a day, but it will be hot and dry. Start early as the wind freshens before noon. Bring sunscreen, bathing suit and camera. Here, the interplay of light and water and the bounty of island colors and fragrances are similar to West Maui, but impart a unique personality because of the different geographic location. For mile-by-mile pictorial details, see *Sunny South Maui*, by A. K. Kepler (Mutual Publishing Co.).

Kamaole II Beach Park, Kihei.

Wailea Beach.

"Lei-d" ladies.Slide

Maui Inter-Continental Wailea

Wailea Point ancient historic site.

Maui Inter-Continental Wailea

Watch for Santa in December!

Maui Inter-Continental Wailea

Lei Contest (May   1).

138

Molokini Island, aerial.

Snorkelers at Molokini.

Makena shoreline.

Ulua Beach, Wailea.

Maui's last lava flow (1790).

Ancient village sites: only for hikers.

UPCOUNTRY AND HALEAKALA

Although a dawn visit to Maui's 10,020-foot summit is justifiably world renowned, this awe-inspiring mountain is spectacular any time. Mornings are clearest but sunsets can also be stunning. Remember to dress appropriately—it is generally windy and cold but may be glaringly hot. The sun rises around 6:50 a.m. in winter, 5:50 in summer. Allow at least two hours driving from Kaanapali. Fill up with gasoline in Pukalani, and bring sunglasses, a jacket, food and water if you plan to spend more than a few minutes at the summit.

A visit to Haleakala Crater, with its lunar beauty, sweeping volcanic panoramas, cliff-girt caldera, fog cloaked escarpments, vast cindery expanses and frozen rivers of lava, is a priceless experience. En route to the summit you pass through "upcountry," with its fields of proteas and carnations, pastoral scenes, "aerial" panoramas of four neighbor islands, and houses with chimneys. Higher elevations bring alpine vegetation, *nene* geese, silverswords, trails, and plenty of information at the National Park Headquarters. If you plan to stay overnight in the crater, make reservations months in advance and don't forget your boots. For detailed descriptions see Haleakala: A Guide to the Mountain by C. B. and A. K. Kepler (Mutual Publishing)

Makawao Library with jacaranda tree.

Horses graze on mid-elevation slopes.

Pukalani Junction: turn left for Haleakala's summit.

A box of renowned Kula onions.

Pastures, Ulupalakua Ranch.

Tedeschi Vineyards' wine-tasting room.

Cameron Kepler

140

Alpine shrubland and *nene* sign.

Science City and silversword.

Inside the Crater: Pele's Paint Pot.

National Park fence and Waikamoi Preserve

Enjoying winter snow at 10,000 feet.

Rain forest, Koolau Forest Reserve.

INDEX

ABOUT THE AUTHOR

Dr. Angela Kay Kepler, a naturalized New Zealander, was born in Australia in 1943. A writer, photographer, field biologist, biological illustrator, and environmental consultant, she holds degrees from the University of Canterbury (New Zealand), University of Hawaii (Honolulu), and cornell University (New York). She also spent one year as a post-doctoral student at Oxford University, England.

Kay first came to Hawaii as an East-West Center foreign student in 1964. Over the last 27 years she has authored 12 books and numerous scientific publications, written newspaper columns on biological and cultural aspects of the Hawaiian Islands, and contributed regular articles and photos to island publications. She and her husband, separately and together, have conducted forest bird and plant surveys, seabird studies and endangered species research in Hawaii and other Pacific islands, the mainland U.S., Alaska, the West Indies, and New Zealand. They have hiked, camped, worked or canoed throughout Hawaii's mountains, lowlands, and coastlines, and traveled in over 60 countries.

Kay is actively involved with Pacific research and conservation. She has visited several uninhabited and remote Pacific atolls on international expeditions of several months' duration.

The Kepler family includes two adopted daughters, Sylvelin and Leilani.